WISCONSIN GERRYMANDERING:
THE FIGHT FOR PERMANENT FAIR MAPS AND WHY IT MATTERS

BY TIM CULLEN

Copyright © 2024 Tim Cullen

All rights reserved. No part of this publication may be reproduced, distributed, or transmitted in any form or by any means, including photocopying, recording, digital scanning, or other electronic or mechanical methods, without the prior written permission of the publisher, except in the case of brief quotations embodied in critical reviews and certain other noncommercial uses permitted by copyright law. For permission requests or other information, please send correspondence to the following address:

Little Creek Press
5341 Sunny Ridge Road
Mineral Point, WI 53565

ORDERING INFORMATION
Quantity sales. Special discounts are available on quantity purchases by corporations, associations, and others. For details, contact info@littlecreekpress.com

Orders by US trade bookstores and wholesalers.
Please contact Little Creek Press or Ingram for details.

Printed in the United States of America

Cataloging-in-Publication Data
Name: Tim Cullen, author
Title: Wisconsin Gerrymandering:
The Fight for Permanent Fair Maps and Why It Matters
Description: Mineral Point, WI Little Creek Press, 2024
Identifiers: LCCN: 2024912200 | ISBN: 978-1-955656-76-4
Classification: POLITICAL SCIENCE / American Government / State
POLITICAL SCIENCE / Corruption & Misconduct
POLITICAL SCIENCE / Political Process / Campaigns & Elections
HISTORY / United States / State & Local / Midwest (IA, IL, IN, KS, MI, MN, MO, ND, NE, OH, SD, WI)

Book design by Little Creek Press

TABLE OF CONTENTS

ABOUT THE AUTHOR................................1

PREFACE..2

1. Governor Gerry and the Salamander:
   What Gerrymandering Is and Isn't................5

2. Gerrymandering Tools: Packing and Cracking, Islands,
   Racial Gerrymandering, Prison Gerrymandering,
   Zig and Zagging the Lines, and Pieces of Pie........21

3. The History of Redistricting in Wisconsin,
   1787 Through the 1950s..........................39

4. Reapportionment Since the 1960 Census:
   Redistricting in the Era of One Person, One Vote.....51

5. 1974 and 1978: Running for the State Senate
   in a District Gerrymandered Against My Party.......61

6. 2011: The Year Gerrymandered Maps by One Party
   Came to Wisconsin and How It Relates to Act 10.....71

7. Dale and Me....................................79

8. February 19, 2024: A Day to Celebrate—
   The People Won!................................85

9. How to End Gerrymandering......................97

10. America's Future..............................103

ACKNOWLEDGMENTS..............................107

APPENDIX......................................110

BIBLIOGRAPHY..................................138

ABOUT THE AUTHOR

Photo credit: Loren Fellows

Tim Cullen was born and raised in Janesville, Wisconsin. Cullen graduated from UW–Whitewater with a major in political science and a minor in history. The first election he won was to the Janesville City Council in 1970. Four years later, Cullen was elected to the state senate as a Democrat at the age of thirty. He went on to become Senate Majority Leader from 1982 to 1987, and in 1987 he became Secretary of the Department of Health and Social Services under Governor Tommy Thompson. Cullen took a job in 1988 with Blue Cross and worked with them for the next 20 years. He served a term on the School District of Janesville School Board from 2007 to 2010. In 2010, he decided to run for his old senate seat. He was elected and served until 2015. Today Cullen still lives in Janesville and spends his time working with the three foundations he started.

Cullen will equally split all profits from this book to the Janesville Multicultural Teachers Scholarship Fund, which he started in 2008, and Beloit's similar scholarship program, Grow Your Own. The sole purpose of these programs is to raise money for college scholarships for students and adults of color. The goal is to support those students who wish to become teachers and are willing to return to Janesville or Beloit to teach. The goal of the foundations is to make the teacher corps look more like the students they teach.

PREFACE

For a glaring example of the corrosive effect of gerrymandering on democracy—gerrymandering being the manipulation of boundaries of electoral districts to favor one political party—you need look no further than the 2010 and 2012 state assembly races in Wisconsin.

In 2010, a very good year for Republicans in the state, the party received about 250,000 more votes statewide in assembly races than Democrats. As one might expect, the Republicans won 60 of the 99 seats, giving them a 60–39 majority in the Wisconsin Assembly.[1]

Prior to the 2012 election, Wisconsin's legislative maps were redrawn. It turned out 2012 was a good year for Democrats at the polls. The party's assembly candidates received about 170,000 more votes statewide than Republicans, a 420,000-vote swing to the Democrats from two years earlier.[2] The logical assumption is that Wisconsin Democrats gained a dramatic number of assembly seats, perhaps a majority.

Not exactly.

The assembly district maps had been so carefully redrawn behind closed doors by partisan Republican attorneys that the Republicans retained their exact 60–39 majority in the assembly despite losing more than 400,000 votes.[3]

That, in a nutshell, is gerrymandering.

I wrote this book because gerrymandering has greatly influenced elections, politics, and, not least, public policy in Wisconsin since the 2010 election, which put Republicans in control of state government. Their 2011 redrawing of the legislative maps was the first partisan gerrymander in Wisconsin in over 60 years. A decade later, the state supreme court endorsed those maps in a 2022 decision, justifying it under the "least change" principle.

Translated into common, understandable language, it meant the court approved another ten years of gerrymandered maps.

I have been involved in fighting gerrymandering since 2009, when, along with others, I urged the Democratic majority in the state legislature to adopt a nonpartisan redistricting plan in the manner of our neighboring state of Iowa. The Democrats could have done it. They controlled the senate and assembly, and Democrat Jim Doyle was governor. But they did not. Republicans took control in the 2010 election, and we know what happened next.

Starting in 2011, people would frequently ask me something like, "How and why does this gerrymander thing happen?" This book is my attempt to answer that question and others as well.

I thought it was time to put in one document the history of this undemocratic (that is with a small "d") act, with an emphasis on my home state of Wisconsin, but with a look, too, at the larger context. Republicans are not the only ones who use gerrymandering. Several states have a Democratic gerrymander. My hope when I started writing was to provide a historical perspective, and this book includes a history of reapportionment in Wisconsin, which, to my surprise, dates to before statehood. I could find no mention of gerrymandering back then, but what occurred "feels" like gerrymandering.

I examine the involvement of the courts (or their refusal to get involved) at both the state and federal levels, along with how redistricting was handled and mishandled for partisan gain over the decades by legislators and governors.

I write mainly about redistricting since 1960, with a particular focus on the last 13 years in Wisconsin, which saw a gerrymander become law in 2011 and then be overturned in 2024.

The events of 2023–2024 are looked at in detail because they impact our lives now and will continue to until 2031, when the new census numbers may impact the maps, unless some other court action occurs.

I also address how to fix the gerrymander threat in future years. The bottom line is that we need to take map drawing out of the hands of the legislature. Legislators have exhibited a never-ending willingness to gerrymander when they have the power to do it.

It's not a political issue; it's an abuse of power issue.

---

[1] Matt Rothschild, 12 *Ways to Save Democracy in Wisconsin* (Wisconsin: University of Wisconsin Press; First Edition, 2021).
[2] Ibid.
[3] Ibid.

CHAPTER 1
Governor Gerry and the Salamander: What Gerrymandering Is and Isn't

Webster's New World Dictionary of the American Language defines *gerrymandering* as "the redistricting of voting districts to the advantage of one party." Redistricting is the process by which states adjust the boundaries of congressional, state legislative, and local electoral districts to account for shifts in population (according to the latest census). Because the census is done every ten years, redistricting is done every ten years.

What we today call gerrymandering started before 1812, but the actual word *gerrymandering* was first seen publicly as the title of a drawing of a Massachusetts senate district by Elkanah Tisdale appearing in the *Boston Gazette* on March 26, 1812.[4]

The Massachusetts Legislature was redrawing its legislative maps (redistricting) in 1812, following the 1810 census. The only purpose was to change district lines to adjust for population changes that occurred during the previous ten years so that, as closely as possible, every district would have the same number of people. This was seldom an actual goal in most or all of America until ordered by a U.S. Supreme Court decision in 1962.

Elbridge Gerry was the governor of Massachusetts in 1812. Gerry lived from 1744 to 1814. He was elected vice president of the United States under James Madison in November 1812 but died shortly after in November 1814. His last name is pronounced with a hard G, although almost everyone pronounces "gerrymandering" with a soft G. Should we be pronouncing it with a hard G? This matter will not keep you awake tonight, but I just had to raise it.

The partisan legislative map drawers in Massachusetts drew some strange-looking districts that year, which Governor Gerry

Massachusetts Governor Elbridge Gerry. Photo credit: James Bogle

approved. One of the district's shapes was so unusual that it was described as looking like a salamander. Illustrator Elkanah Tisdale drew a picture of the district with wings and scales, which appeared on March 26, 1812, in the *Boston Gazette* headlined "The Gerry-mander."[5] The name has stuck to this day.

I must give Massachusetts credit for being consistent—even today they have a gerrymandered legislative map.

While redistricting must comply with previous federal and state court decisions and legislative directives, maps can be drawn that comply with all of these legal requirements *and* also be a gerrymander. This reality must be acknowledged. You will hear

Tisdale's "The Gerry-mander."
Photo credit: Wikimedia Commons

elected officials attempt to change the subject by talking about how their maps "comply with all federal and state requirements." This can be true, but those maps can also still be gerrymandered and take away the value of a citizen's vote.

I would use "legal corruption" as a definition for gerrymandering. *Corruption* is a big, serious word that I do not use lightly.

Why is gerrymandering corrupt? Its intended result is that the majority party, by way of the maps they themselves draw, almost certainly guarantees themselves majority control of the legislature (by very large margins) for the decade. So legislators, by their one vote to enact a gerrymandered legislative district map, do the following:

- They guarantee themselves a job for the following ten years. How many of you can guarantee, by your own action, that you will keep your current job for the next ten years? My guess is only if you are the owner. In Wisconsin, legislators are paid $57,408 per year plus a per diem for every day they are in Madison (whether they're there for ten minutes or ten hours!).[6]
- It guarantees ten more years of growth in their pension.
- It guarantees health insurance for the legislator and their family for ten years.

Not bad, huh? Their pay and per diem will likely increase at least once or twice during the ten years. These salaries and per diem rates are increased by a legislative committee controlled by the majority party.

How much has all of this raised your blood pressure? My apologies.

I think all of this describes "corrupt" behavior. The dictionary defines *corrupt* as "something corrupted, as an improperly altered word or text." There are other definitions in the dictionary, but I thought this one was the most relevant one for action that involved a document. In the case of gerrymandering, the documents are maps.

A fundamental question is, "How can a person know that Wisconsin is gerrymandered?" The answer is that if the statewide elections, such as governor or president, are very close races regardless of whether a Republican or Democrat wins, but the same party wins 60 percent or more of state legislative races, election after election, that is an indication of a gerrymander. This is what we have seen in Wisconsin since 2012.

Wisconsin citizens in 32 counties have expressed their strong opposition to gerrymandering. These counties passed non-binding referendums opposing gerrymanders by large margins, most by margins of around 70–30 percent. My home county of Rock passed it 80–20 percent. Fifty-six county boards passed resolutions supporting fair maps. These numbers make clear that more than just Democrats oppose gerrymandering. An overwhelming majority of citizens have figured this out and don't like it.

People who are not spending their lives studying gerrymandering will understandably think it is either always the Democrats or always the Republicans doing it. Gerrymandering can only occur in a state when one of the political parties controls the governorship and both houses of the legislature in the year following the census. So either the Democrats or Republicans are blamed in whatever state you reside if a gerrymander occurs.

The reality is that gerrymandering is the abuse of power. Whichever political party has total control in a state can't help themselves. They will abuse their power and draw maps that zig and zag to carve districts that deliver a large majority of votes (60–70 percent) for their party. The districts are often carved in such a way that not all parts of the district are even connected. Remember the salamander! They create "islands" of areas that are not connected to the main area of the district. With new, non-gerrymandered maps, this practice will end. The state supreme court recently found these noncontiguous "islands" unconstitutional. Several districts were noncontiguous in 2023.

When it comes to understanding what any redistricting map is all about, we always need to know the result of the map (which party benefits). The people who draw the map know. The rest of us deserve to know, too.

To further explain gerrymandering, I should discuss the national census and its role in redistricting (and, therefore, sometimes gerrymandering).

Every ten years, the federal government conducts a nationwide census to collect data that reveals the population changes in each legislative district, which can then be compared to the population of that district ten years earlier. Redistricting is required every ten years after the census because Article 1, Section 2 of the U.S. Constitution and Section 2 of the 14th Amendment of the U.S. Constitution (see Appendix) require it. The U.S. census is done every ten years in the years ending in zero. This is why the redrawing of district lines begins every ten years in the year ending in one.

The Wisconsin Assembly must have between 54 and 100 districts, and the senate must have no less than one-quarter and no more than one-third of the assembly, according to Article IV of the state constitution. The current map complies with this, with 33 state senate districts and 99 assembly districts.

The current population of each district will determine whether districts need to add or subtract citizens by adding or subtracting land so that each district holds approximately the statewide average number of citizens. This is the sole purpose and role of this part of the census process. The result will be that each district will have, as near as possible, an equal number of citizens.

State legislative districts are permitted to deviate somewhat from reaching perfect population equality in order to accomplish traditional districting objectives, including preserving the integrity of political subdivisions, maintaining communities of interest, and creating geographic compactness.

The equal population requirement has been determined to be a deviation of population between legislative districts of 10 percent or less. Wisconsin maps have easily met this 10 percent threshold. This is again proof that gerrymandering can meet "legal requirements" and also be a gerrymander. This was the case in the 2011 and 2022 gerrymandered maps. People intent on gerrymandering can do it while complying with legal requirements. The chart below from the Legislative Reference Bureau shows Wisconsin's population deviation:

Relative Population Deviation for Wisconsin	
1982	1.74%
1992	0.91%
2002	1.59%
2011	0.90%[7]

Incredible. Federal judges drew up the 1982, 1992, and 2002 maps, and they were not gerrymandered. No credible person ever said they were. Then came 2011 and the Republican gerrymander. The gerrymandered map did the best job of all four decades of having the least deviation from perfection.

This is one of the best examples of a clear case in which you can comply with court-ordered standards of redistricting and also gerrymander.

The census and the equal population requirement are intended to meet the goal of equal representation, or as it is often called, "one person, one vote." Before women had the right to vote, it was called "one man, one vote." The census also impacts many federal programs.

On the surface, this process is good for democracy. But now enters the temptation to gerrymander.

As Wisconsin's redistricting in 2011 shows, a map of a district can be drawn with purely partisan goals, which is bad for democracy, as long as it has the required number of citizens in each district. Gerrymandering results in some incredible zigging and zagging of areas to get not just an equal number of citizens but a large majority of majority party voters in a large majority of the legislative districts.

You may be asking, "How do the map drawers know how people vote?" The answer is that they look at previous results in a ward and, using today's technology, can find out the value of your home, what kind of car you drive, what types of media and news outlets you pay attention to, etc. All that adds to the composite picture of how you vote.

The lines of the districts, including the use of "islands," are drawn with one goal in mind: create at least a 60 percent majority party-leaning district.

The other necessity for the map drawers (gerrymanderers) is to stuff as many minority party voters into as few other districts as possible. What then happens is the minority party's districts are even safer for the minority party than the majority party's drawn districts are for the majority party. The majority party loves legislative districts that are 80 percent minority party voters because it means fewer minority party voters in other districts. And the truth is that some minority party legislators also like this because it means they can keep their job for another ten years. They will never, however, have the power to pass legislation because, with gerrymandering, they will always be in the minority party.

A residual—and undemocratic—effect of gerrymandering is that only the primary elections matter. General elections nearly always have a larger voter turnout than primary elections. However, in gerrymandered states, the only election that is competitive and actually matters is the primary.

The general election in gerrymandered districts is decided the day the maps are drawn. The only rare exception to this is when there is a landslide election win for the minority party. This has happened in Wisconsin only once in the last 50 years—in 1974, the year I benefited from it.

What are some consequences? The big one is that the incumbents in these seats want to avoid a primary opponent. (The majority party holds a majority of these seats, and the minority party holds a minority of these seats.)

The safest way to avoid a primary opponent is to stick with your base, and usually that includes supporting their extreme views. Do nothing that will get you called a "compromiser" or a "moderate." Generally, these base citizens in each party vote in big numbers in the primary.

There can be a huge impact on legislators who don't agree (vote) with their party's leadership. If elected officials move to the views of the extreme wing of their own party and leadership, they will likely avoid a primary. Not being far enough to the left or right can lead to an incumbent's own leadership recruiting and supporting a primary opponent for them in their own party. Bullying isn't just for grade schoolers. A candidate who is more likely to support the base's extreme views will be chosen to run against you in the primary if the incumbent doesn't fall into line. Gerrymandering causes a candidate in the majority party to feel safe in the general election but greatly affects the primary. Not straying from leadership views guarantees no primary opponent (at least not a serious one) and job security for another ten years.

This behavior makes compromise almost impossible. Enter hyper-partisanship! Voters in the political middle—and there are many—are left voiceless.

A huge consequence of attaining fair maps is that the general election in November matters again. This means that legislators need to pay attention to the views of a much larger number of their constituents. One of the ways to do this is to look for compromises with the other party to get something passed into law. Legislation that is far to the left or right would be hard to pass.

Legislative leaders will be unable to find primary opponents for their party's members as they have in Wisconsin with a gerrymander. These likely far-left or far-right candidates would unlikely be able to win a general election. That legislative leader, were they to do this, could reduce their caucus by one. The caucus then may well look for a new leader.

Clearly, there are numerous reasons why fair maps matter.

The Wisconsin Supreme Court and federal judges have generally, over the past 60 years, focused on past court and legislative actions that led to several reapportionment guidelines being followed now. They include the following:

- Nearly equal populations in each assembly and senate district.
- Eliminate "islands" so that the entire legislative district is contiguous.
- Try not to unnecessarily split up cities, towns, and villages into two or more different districts for partisan reasons.

While the above guidelines have good intentions—and I certainly agree with them—districts that make great progress on *all* of the above can still be gerrymandered. Partisan map drawers know exactly how to do this and have done it.

The latest Wisconsin Supreme Court ruling in December 2023 declared the 2022 maps unconstitutional. Through this decision, gerrymanderers have not lost their ability to draw district lines that zig and zag, but they have lost one of their most helpful tools—islands. (I address this term more in Chapter 2.)

The League of Women Voters of Wisconsin (LWV) played a key role in the victorious fight against gerrymandering in Wisconsin. The LWV put out an excellent brochure that I want to share with you. Gerrymandering can be a difficult issue to understand in its entirety, but voters in a democracy need to know the harms of gerrymandering. The brochure states in straightforward language the detriments of gerrymandering. The following are their key points:

Elected officials do not have to listen to voters and are more loyal to their party and their donors. Legislators in gerrymandered districts are almost guaranteed re-election, making them less accountable to voters.

Gerrymandering is often used when re-election is threatened. Legislators who are in danger of losing an election can be redistricted by the party to enhance their chances of winning. (This, of course, only applies to legislators in the majority party. Minority party legislators are also safe … but safe deep in the minority!)

Polarization increases. Compromise is lost. In gerrymandered districts, candidates are forced into extreme positions of their party and their donors. (Being called a "compromiser" or a "moderate" can get you a primary. Hence the LWV word *forced*.)

Transparency to voters is lost. Wisconsin's current maps (the ones that had been in place since 2011 and have recently been replaced under Act 94) were drawn by lawyers in locked rooms, and (majority party) legislators had to swear secrecy to see their district. (And that is all they saw. They did not see the statewide map.) Communication among legislators was prohibited. (I was in that legislature, and this lasted about ten minutes.)

Gerrymandering is expensive. Millions of tax dollars are spent to hire lawyers (and other expert map drawers from around the country) to draw the maps and to defend them in court battles. Since the 1980s, Iowa has utilized nonpartisan staff to draw undisputed maps at negligible costs. (The gerrymandered maps of 2011, which were largely kept in place by the state supreme court, in 2022 cost taxpayers $2 million. The cost in 2023–2024 for the people hired by the court to draft new maps did not exceed $500,000. So the taxpayers paid four times as much to get maps that greatly diminished the value of their votes as they paid to get maps that restored the value of their vote. No wonder taxpayers are so angry and skeptical of how their government spends their money.)[8]

I agree with every item in the LWV brochure. My comments are in parentheses.

Give Matt Rothschild credit for his definition of *gerrymandering* in his book *12 Ways to Save Democracy in Wisconsin*. He defines it as "the manipulative drawing of district maps to give an advantage to the political party in power." He also very accurately refers to political power as "an intoxicating drug."[9]

I also read in Matt's book that Dr. Martin Luther King Jr. is one of his favorite leaders in our nation's history. I have this in common with him. However, we also agree that we don't agree with one of Dr. King's most famous quotes: "The arc of the moral universe is long, but it bends toward justice."

I agree with Matt's view that "history is not an arc; it is a zigzag."[10]

I admire the message that Dr. King was trying to address, except the "arc" part.

I mention this matter because as I researched and wrote this book, it was clear to me that the history of the effort to get rid of gerrymandering in Wisconsin was a history of zigs and zags! We have seen a solution for each ten-year cycle, usually having a state or federal court intervene and avoid a gerrymander (1980s, 1990s, 2000, and 2023). The 1970s brought about a remarkable solution: a bipartisan gerrymander. (If "bipartisan" was a human with feelings, it would be terribly hurt to be in the same sentence with "gerrymander.")

I also agree with something else that Matt wrote: "History is not going in one direction. And it is not predetermined. We all, with concerted actions, can affect its direction and outcome."11

Many of us fighting gerrymandering are trying to establish a nonpartisan, Iowa-type process for drawing district maps. Chapter 9 explores this topic further. There have been efforts to create a nonpartisan redistricting process in Wisconsin for over a century, so history is completely clear. The people want to end gerrymandering. It is obviously very difficult to do, and indeed, it has never been done.

It is worth noting that 37 states still leave the map-drawing process to the legislature, and most need the governor's signature like every other piece of legislation. The other 13 states have different ways of redistricting. Iowa is the only state that has a nonpartisan state agency that draws the maps. The other 12 states have some version of a commission. Our goal in Wisconsin is not to create a commission but rather to mirror (although not completely copy) the Iowa system.

Gerrymandering is not the same as issues like public education, taxes, health care, etc. However, a gerrymander can severely affect whether or not these issues are addressed, and if they are addressed, gerrymandering can determine how they are addressed and the outcomes. I believe it is very important to keep this reality in the front of our minds. The two political parties usually have very different views on how to address big issues.

I have come to believe strongly that two of the most overused and misleading words used by politicians and others are *complex* and *complicated*. They can be interchanged in speech.

I wrote about this in my first book, *Ringside Seat*, in 2015. Their overuse and misleading use go way beyond the political world. They're often used in the business world, too, when reporters pose questions, and business leaders explain the problem they are confronted with in an interview, defending why the unsolved problem is not fixed. It is not fixed because it is either "complex" or "complicated," the speakers say. I actually heard one person being interviewed use them both in the same sentence in answer to a question.

In truth, the solution needed to solve whatever problem is being discussed is usually not particularly difficult, and the problem might have a fairly obvious solution or at least a solution that can be identified.

What is really going on is that the solution is "politically complex" or "politically complicated" for them to explain. In other words, they're worried about losing their next election! Business leaders worry that the solution might hurt their stock prices or risk their jobs. Implementing the needed action is then delayed as they hope for a miracle action that will fix the problem and allow them to avoid blame.

My suggestion to you as you read about gerrymandering (or other issues in front of politicians) is to listen for one or both of these words. If you are talking to your elected officials, listen for these words and then ask for a further explanation so you do not just accept their one-word explanation.

It seems like several times a week, I hear these words used, and they just jump out at me.

In Wisconsin, the non-gerrymandered 2024 map will hopefully bring a new reality of quite narrow majorities in both houses of the legislature and maybe see each party controlling one house of the legislature. This possible situation would mean that compromise and cooperation would be necessary to get anything done. Wouldn't that be nice to see?

---

[4] Erick Trickey, "Where Did the Term 'Gerrymandering' Come From?" *Smithsonian* Magazine, July 20, 2017, https://www.smithsonianmag.com/history/where-did-term-gerrymander-come-180964118/.

[5] Ibid.

[6] Wisconsin Legislative Reference Bureau, LRB Reports, "Salaries of State Elected Officials, 2023," Volume 7, Number 5, February 2023: 2, https://docs.legis.wisconsin.gov/misc/lrb/lrb_reports/elected_official_salaries_2023_7_5.pdf.

[7] Michael Gallagher, Joseph Kreye, and Staci Duros, PhD. *Redistricting in Wisconsin 2020: The LRB Guidebook*, Wisconsin Legislative Reference Bureau, Wisconsin Elections Project, vol.1, no. 2, 2020, 10, https://docs.legis.wisconsin.gov/misc/lrb/wisconsin_elections_project/redistricting_wisconsin_2020_1_2.pdf.

[8] League of Women Voters, *Fair Maps Representation for All* (Brochure).

[9] Matt Rothschild, *12 Ways to Save Democracy in Wisconsin* (Wisconsin: University of Wisconsin Press; First Edition, 2021), 9.

[10] Ibid.

[11] Ibid.

CHAPTER 2

Gerrymandering Tools:
Packing and Cracking, Islands,
Racial Gerrymandering, Prison Gerrymandering,
Zig and Zagging the Lines, and Pieces of Pie

Packing and Cracking

Packing and *cracking* are two words often used to describe how maps are drawn to create a gerrymander.

Packing is used to describe putting as many minority party voters into as few districts as possible. This leaves the majority of districts heavily favoring the majority party.

"Self-packing" is a term used by some Republicans when they are accused of gerrymandering. Republicans claim (with a straight face) that Democrats created their own electoral failures because they self-pack, meaning there are too many Democrats living in just a few areas. They assert that Democrats dilute their own votes by packing themselves into large cities (Madison, Milwaukee, etc.), which causes them to have huge margins of victory there but, consequently, not many Democratic voters in other areas of the state. It is a purposely dishonest argument to distract from the fact that they have gerrymandered. The problem with this argument is that Republicans also self-pack in suburban Milwaukee (in the so-called WOW counties of Waukesha, Ozaukee, and Washington). And how do they explain or blame the Democrats for all the zigging and zagging of district lines or using "prison gerrymandering" and "islands" to draw gerrymandered districts in other areas of Wisconsin? Self-packing is a weak argument.

Cracking means splitting strong minority party cities or areas into two nearby districts. This breaks up a strong minority party area, creating two districts that the majority party can win and one less minority party district.

Islands

You may be wondering what islands have to do with gerrymandering. Islands are supposed to be vacation spots in oceans in warm weather climates, right? Their other identity is better known following the Wisconsin Supreme Court decision of December 22, 2023.

Islands are another disgusting gerrymandering tactic used to keep the majority party in power for ten more years. Islands occur when a legislative district has parts that are completely detached from the rest of the district (like an island is detached from the mainland). This means the district is "noncontiguous" to use the court's and constitution's language, and noncontiguous means unconstitutional. Another way to look at this is if the incumbent legislator is in the island area, they must drive through someone else's district to get to another part of their district.

On December 22, 2023, the Wisconsin Supreme Court ruled on a case involving reapportionment. The court declared the state legislative maps unconstitutional and ordered new maps to be in place for the 2024 elections. The core of the decision was that the maps violated a state constitutional requirement that legislative districts must be contiguous.[12] In plain English, this means the constitution says, "no islands." This little-known issue had become the central issue in the court's decision.

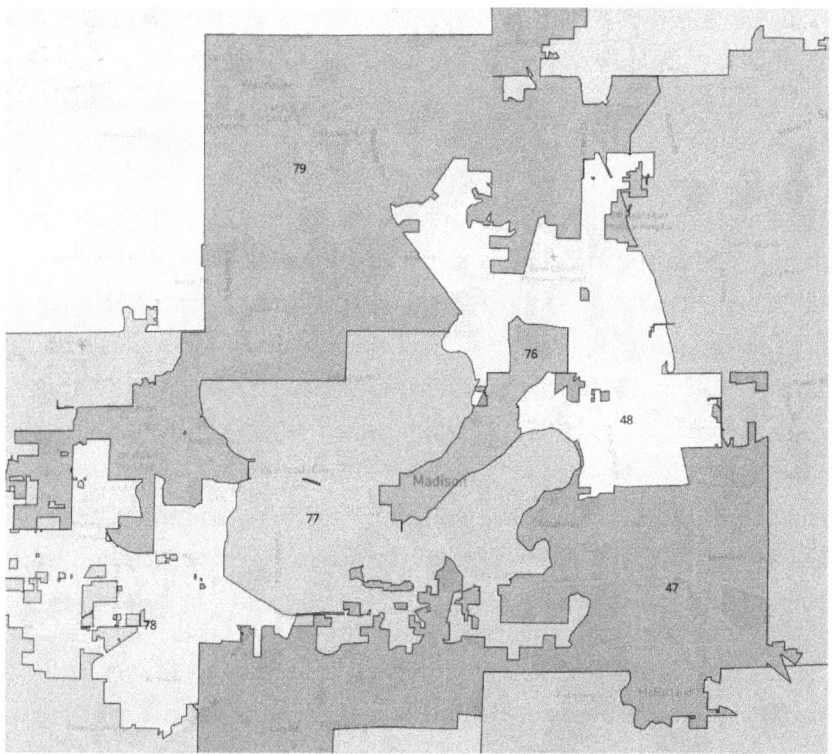

Example of non-contiguous "islands" in Dane County Assembly District Map 2022. Photo credit: Legislative Technology Services Bureau and Campaign Legal Center

This island problem was widespread in the maps used for the 2022 elections. How bad was it? The numbers tell the story. At least 50 of the 99 assembly seats and at least 20 of the 33 state senate seats had islands.[13]

Contiguity is a state requirement for redistricting and is not a federal issue, meaning that it is not likely that the United States Supreme Court would intervene and overturn or change the decision.

Racial Gerrymandering

Racial gerrymandering is what you are likely thinking it is. It revolves around the idea that voters of a certain race often live in the same area and mostly agree on supporting the same candidate. Cracking and packing often go hand in hand with racial gerrymandering. Packing or cracking for race discrimination is a simple but disgusting process. Packing people of color into one district to prevent that group's chance to win two or more districts is wrong.

Cracking occurs when members of a minority group are split up or spread out into two or more districts, so the likelihood of a person of color winning any district is low. You may think that racially segregated political districts are a thing of the past. But as Deborah Turner said in 2020: "Racial gerrymandering continues to happen, only masked as partisan gerrymandering." Deborah Turner was president of the National League of Women Voters until her death in January 2024. When she said this, she was hosting a panel in the fall of 2020 titled "Racism and Redistricting: How Unfair Maps Impact Communities of Color."

Past court decisions that were intended to increase the opportunity for a person of color to get elected have contributed to the challenges of the issue. The courts had good intentions but also created other consequences.

Here is how I assess this issue. The early concerns were to make sure people of color had a chance to win more than one seat. I was in the state senate from 1975 to 1987. There was never more than one senator of color in the senate.

I served with Black state senators Monroe Swan and Gary George. Senator George followed Senator Swan into the state senate from the same district in Milwaukee.

The issue that has emerged is a dilemma. The question becomes how much does one want to put more Black or Hispanic voters in another state senate seat, and when does that decision create the possibility that a Black or Hispanic candidate will win none of the districts? I am not talking about any specific state senate districts. These are hypothetical senate seats.

The bottom line is how much do you want to risk an almost certain election of a candidate in order to win one or two more? People will have different opinions. I am confident that Black, Hispanic, and possibly other leaders will handle each situation well.

The 14th Amendment to the U.S. Constitution was ratified in 1868, just after the Civil War. The equal protection clause in Section 1 of the 14th Amendment states: "No state shall deny to any person within its jurisdiction the equal protection of the laws."

This clause does not mention race, but since it was adopted just three years after the end of the Civil War, historians have frequently concluded that this amendment is about race.

The bottom line is that racial gerrymandering should be considered a violation of the 14th Amendment of the U.S. Constitution.

Proving racial gerrymandering has been very difficult to do in court. A plaintiff must prove that race was the predominant motivating factor. Basically, if the defendant can show that other factors led to the maps being drawn as they were, racial gerrymandering is very difficult to prove.

What stands out to me about the above is that as in non-racially related gerrymandering, where you can gerrymander while meeting judicial requirements like "equal population" and other requirements from several court cases over many decades, you can also gerrymander for racial reasons and hide behind the court requirements in the drawing of the maps.

The United States has had the 14th and 15th Amendments since their passage in 1868 and 1870. They were intended to protect the rights of people to vote regardless of their "race, color, or previous condition of servitude." Yet nearly 100 years after the passage of the two amendments, the Voting Rights Act (VRA) of 1965 was passed (see Appendix).

How many people who were in one of those groups had difficulty voting or were outright denied the right to vote in those 90-plus years?

The VRA quoted the unmet requirements of the 15th Amendment 95 years after its passing.

Key language in the VRA focuses on whether a standard, practice, or procedure has the *effect* of discriminating against a racial, color, or language minority group.

A redistricting plan can be challenged under Section 2 of the VRA if it results in "vote dilution." This is cracking. To repeat, vote dilution and cracking both refer to carving up a district that, if left whole, would likely elect a minority person. Carving it up results in minority candidates not winning in any of those districts.

All of the above is not enough. The VRA lists three other conditions that must be met, which are called the "Gingles Preconditions."

Those conditions are as follows:

- The minority group must be large enough and compact enough to otherwise create a majority-minority group. Translated, this means less than 50 percent of the group but the largest single group.
- The group is politically cohesive. Translated, this means individuals in the group tend to vote the same way (for the same party).
- The majority group (white people) also votes as a bloc, so in the absence of special circumstances (lawyers would love this), the majority group's preferred candidate would be certain to defeat the minority group's preferred candidate.[14]

Put simply, the VRA, while addressing a serious problem, makes it more difficult to stop the problem behavior. Racial minorities and other marginalized groups have amendments to the U.S. Constitution and legislation on their side. However, the path to equality for them requires a trip through the legal system that, at best, causes delay and, at worst, makes the effort to elect more people of color more difficult.

I've concluded that the map drawers can meet all of the legal requirements of compactness (keeping communities intact), contiguity (no islands), preservation of communities of interest, and preservation of the unity of political subdivisions and still gerrymander.

The U.S. Supreme Court has said that if evidence shows that a map was drafted with concern for following these principles, it may be enough to pass legal muster.

The above reminds me of the example of someone driving down the road and seeing another driver on one side of the road with a car that won't start, waving for help. If the driver going by is concerned for the guy whose car won't start but drives on without stopping, then that is enough.

Prison Gerrymandering

Many of you reading this may be asking yourselves, "What the heck do prisons or prisoners have to do with gerrymandering?" After all, prisoners cannot vote.

What this means is that most of Wisconsin's large prisons are located in relatively sparsely populated areas in central Wisconsin and west near the Mississippi River. One primary purpose of prison gerrymandering is to circumvent the one-person, one-vote court cases from the 1960s.

Here is the gerrymander connection. The inmates in these prisons are counted in the population total of the township, village, or city in which the prison is located. But they cannot vote. So how does this matter? The U.S. Census for everyone is conducted under what they call the "usual residence" rule. In other words, a person's residence is where they live on census day. The first U.S. Census (1790), and every census since, have been conducted using this rule. This prison population makes up a significant percentage of the population in many rural and small communities. However, because prisoners don't vote, the number of eligible voters is lower than in other state assembly and senate seats. This makes voters who live in a district with a prison have their vote carry more weight than in districts without one. This clearly violates the one-person, one-vote rule.

It's interesting to note that Maine and Vermont are the only two states that allow prisoners to vote.

The small town of Anamosa, Iowa, provides an extreme example of how prison gerrymandering gives more political power to people who live in a district with a prison. This is an example in a city, not a state assembly or senate district, but I believe it makes clear how prison gerrymandering works.

In 2005, the city was divided into four wards, each with about 1,400 residents. Each ward elected one city councilman. One of the wards included Anamosa State Penitentiary, which contained 1,300 prisoners who could not, of course, vote. That meant that the remaining 100 residents of the ward had the same amount of political power as the 1,400 citizens of the other three wards.

Anamosa has now eliminated the ward containing the prison, and the 100 residents who live there have been folded into the other wards.

This extreme example of the impact of prison gerrymandering in Anamosa allows us to see how it would work in an assembly seat. Fewer voters in a prison assembly seat will decide election winners than in assembly seats with no prison.

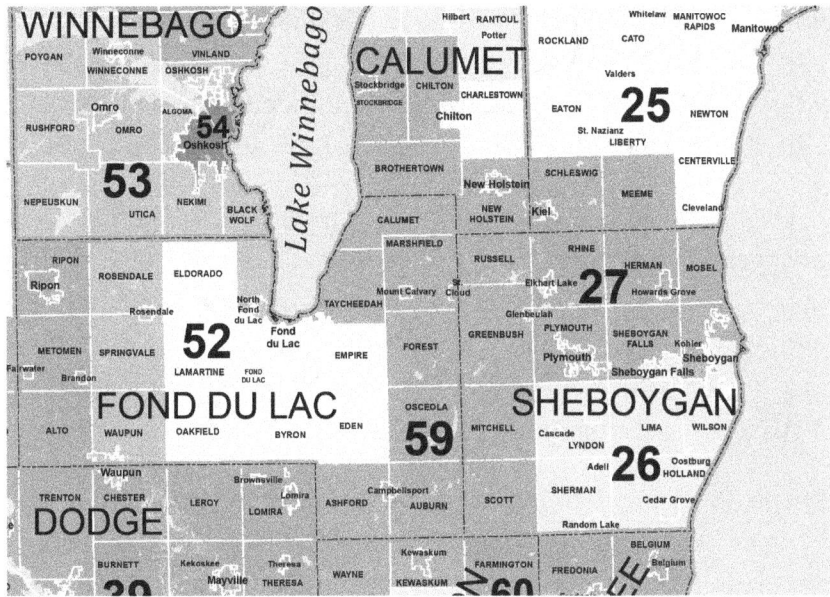

Gerrymandered 53rd Assembly District.
Photo credit: Wisconsin Legislative Technology Services Bureau

The Waupun Correctional Institution is in the 53rd Assembly District. On the map of the district, the prison is at the southern tip of the finger that extends south from the rest of the district. It is not a great leap to speculate that this "finger" is all about getting the prison and, therefore, its population of 1,001 in the 53rd Assembly District.

Wisconsin built its first prison in Waupun in 1853. It has been remodeled and still operates today. The design capacity of the Waupun Correctional Facility as of June 7, 2024, is 882, and 707 prisoners occupy the facility.[15]

Wisconsin abolished the death penalty in 1853. We were the third state to do it. (Michigan and Rhode Island were the first two.) One side effect of this is that a prisoner who may have been executed would likely be sentenced to life without parole, which means more prisoners receive long sentences.

Prison gerrymandering transfers political power away from urban communities (the actual home to many prisoners) to legislators who have prisons in their rural, small-population villages and cities in their districts.

If all the citizens 18 or older can vote, and say 10 percent (the prisoners) cannot vote, then that increases the value of your vote in the district with a prison compared to a citizen's vote in districts without one. The bottom line is that it makes the vote of a citizen in a "prison district" 10 percent more important than the vote in a district without a prison.

Prison gerrymandering has a long history in Wisconsin, and so does the location of almost all of our large prisons in low-population areas. I have been told by two of my Republican friends (Dale Schultz is not one of them) that these prison locations were not an accident nor related to any prison-related issues.

This issue of prison gerrymandering can be fixed. However, the broader issue remains. Wisconsin has overwhelmingly located its prisons in rural small towns, while a substantial percentage of their prisoners do not live in those sparsely populated areas. They live in cities where so much of the population lives. This is a policy question for a governor and a legislature to resolve. The obvious answer is to build new prisons closer to or in urban areas. Unless prisoners are serving life sentences without parole, they will be paroled, and their likelihood of living a crime-free life is much more likely if they return to live with their families. That is more likely if there have been regular visits from their children, spouses, and other friends and family. A closer location makes regular contact much more likely.

Shocking news broke across Wisconsin on June 5, 2024. The warden at the Waupun Correctional Facility and eight other employees were charged with felonies for the mistreatment of prisoners that involved the death of four prisoners. Neither the race of the deceased prisoners nor the race of the people charged with felonies has been disclosed.

This news will hopefully lead to accountability and reform, including closing some of the oldest rural small-town prisons and building them closer to urban Wisconsin. I have observed over my lifetime that it sometimes takes a tragedy to spark needed reform.

Though I can't prove location by location of each of our adult male prisons, I am completely comfortable saying that behind each location decision, there is political pressure from legislators and governors to put a prison in a specific county or community. Why? Jobs, jobs, jobs!

The problem is the above reason has nothing to do with the best policy for good prison administration.

We do not build new prisons in Wisconsin very often. It is a long-term solution but also the only permanent solution.

The Racine Correctional Institution was the last new prison built in southeast Wisconsin in Sturtevant, a small community west of Racine. It opened in 1991. This occurred during the administration of Governor Tommy Thompson, whom I have known for over 50 years but got to know better when we served as legislative leaders from 1982 to 1986. In 1987 and 1988, I served as Secretary of the Department of Health and Social Services in Thompson's administration, and at that time, Corrections was a part of the DHSS. The location of the new prison in southeast Wisconsin was a big step toward locating prisons in southeast Wisconsin.

The placement of the prison was good for many of the inmates and their families, and the politics (it always plays a role) of that location worked for the governor, too. It was located in a Republican state representative's district. Democratic state Senator Joe Strohl,

Tommy G. Thompson Governor of Wisconsin 1987–2001. Photo credit: UW System

the Senate Majority Leader who Thompson needed to work with (along with other Democrats who controlled the senate), would be pleased to get a prison in his district. Good public policy won, too, because of the location in southeast Wisconsin.

This has nothing to do with gerrymandering, but how Governor Thompson worked this out is just one example that explains why he is the longest-serving governor in Wisconsin history. He served 14 years and the beginning of a 15th year. No other governor in

Wisconsin state history has served more than eight years.

It should also be noted that state legislators generally want prisons in their districts, especially rural districts, because that means jobs. Another bad public policy result, however, is that if you locate the prison in rural, small-town Wisconsin, the staff largely hired from those areas will be overwhelmingly white. Statistics say that a number of the prisoners will be non-white. It is also hard to hire corrections officers of color who want to live in small, rural communities. What is the result? The guards and the prisoners will need to be with people with whom neither group is familiar.

This issue also has nothing to do with gerrymandering, but it is a consequence of making decisions for bad reasons in the first place.

I had not heard much about prison gerrymandering while I was involved in this issue for at least 15 years. Now, as I learn more and more, I have come to believe that the side issues may be as important to address as the impact of prison gerrymandering on legislative seats.

Prison gerrymandering has a significant impact on economics, too.

The federal census determines the flow of federal dollars to local districts on a per capita basis. Therefore, if a prisoner from southeast Wisconsin is sent to a prison in a small community in rural Wisconsin, the prison area gets credit for the prisoners in the aid formula despite the pretty clear reality that the home community of the prisoner needs the federal dollars more. The prisoners, as a practical matter, do not live in the community of the prison. The prisoner does not need streets fixed, their trash picked up, police, fire protection, public schools, etc. The prisoners' costs for incarceration are paid from the budget of the State Department of Corrections. So all of us pay for the costs of the prisoners, including the citizens in the community where the prison is located. Prisons, however, benefit from the federal aid with no local costs.

Another issue is that the population of the prison is set in the year following the census. The prisoner could be paroled one year later, but the community gets to count the prisoner for the next nine years. The bigger reality is the community can count all prisoners released over nine years for federal aid.

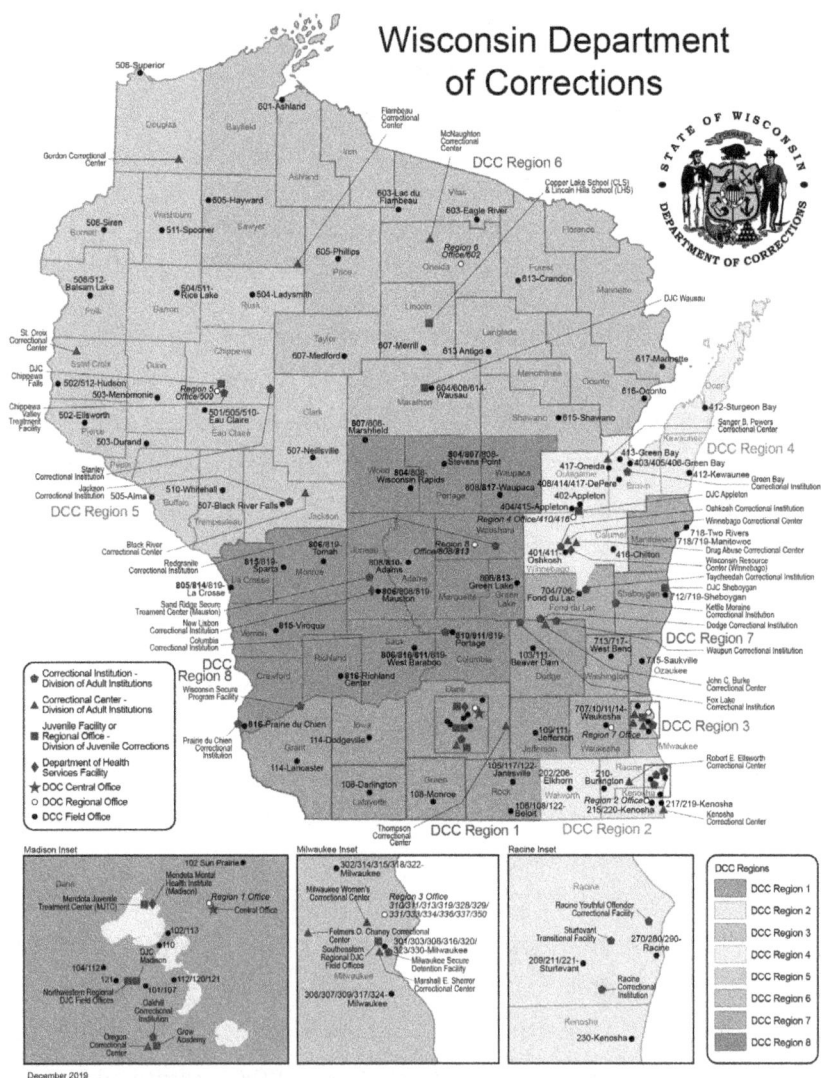

Wisconsin DOC prison locations. Photo credit: Wisconsin Department of Corrections

How do we fix this? Well, 13 states have banned prison gerrymandering: California, Colorado, Connecticut, Delaware, Illinois, Maryland, Massachusetts, Montana, Nevada, New Jersey, New York, Virginia, and Washington. Efforts are ongoing to abolish it in Michigan, Minnesota, and Pennsylvania.

We could end prison gerrymandering in Wisconsin if the legislature passes a law that does so and the governor signs it. It has been tried unsuccessfully in the past.

The main contention in lawsuits in other states is that it violates the one-person, one-vote principle of the 14th Amendment to the U.S. Constitution.

It will likely take total Democratic control of state government for this ban to pass. At the end of the day, this is a matter of raw politics. Prison gerrymandering disproportionately helps Republicans and hurts Democrats.

Zig and Zagging

Another way to gerrymander is to use "zig and zagging" with the legislative district lines. One thing is clear to me. Every, and I mean every, zig and zag has the purpose of adding voters or getting rid of voters the majority party needs to create their gerrymander.

How do they know what areas to zig around or zag to include? Data. They can easily get the past voting pattern of any area of the state, city, ward, village, or township. They can find out the vehicle you drive, magazines you read, etc. This information forms a picture of how you are likely to vote. Zig and zagging helps to pack and crack, which are gerrymandering tactics I discussed earlier.

Pieces of Pie

One other way to gerrymander can be best seen by looking at the Democratic gerrymander in Illinois. This tactic has been called "pieces of pie."

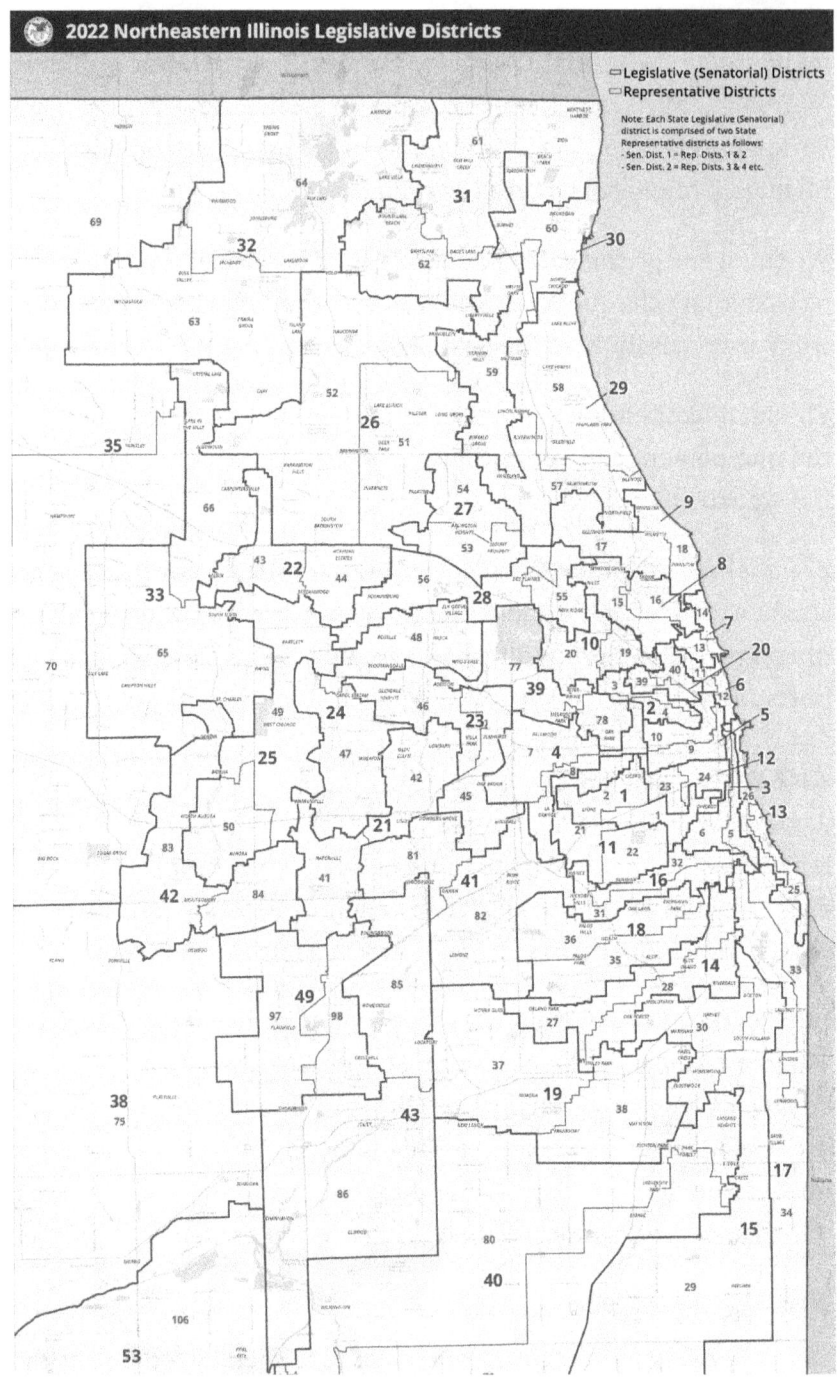

"Pieces of pie" gerrymandering tool used by Democratic legislators in Illinois in 2022. Photo credit: Illinois State Board of Elections

The city of Chicago usually votes overwhelmingly Democrat, sometimes as high as 80 percent. Many Democratic voters are put in legislative districts around Chicago. They put these voters in suburban districts that almost always vote Republican. The shape of this often looks like a piece of pie. Hence the name. The "point" on the piece of pie is in Chicago, and all of the Democratic voters make the legislative district potentially winnable.

Gerrymandering rules to follow: The majority party creates safe districts for themselves—but not too safe. Sixty to 70 percent is safe enough. They do not want 75–80 percent because this "wastes" voters who could be used to help a neighboring district go to the majority party.

The opposite applies when it comes to the districts that the minority party will win. The majority will stuff those districts with as many minority party voters as possible. Seventy-five percent is better than 70, and so on.

Zig and zagging is the preferred tool to accomplish this. Islands (or noncontiguous districts) were used to help accomplish this in the past until the Wisconsin Supreme Court declared them unconstitutional in December 2023.

---

[12] *Rebecca Clarke v. Wisconsin Elections Commission*, 2023AP1399-OA, Wisconsin Supreme Court. December 22, 2023: 3.

[13] Ibid., 2.

[14] *Thornburg v. Gingles*, 478 U.S. 30 (1986), 478.

[15] Wisconsin Department of Corrections, DOC-302, "Persons in Our Care," https://doc.wi.gov/DataResearch/WeeklyPopulationReports/06142024.pdf.

CHAPTER 3

The History of Redistricting in Wisconsin, 1787 Through the 1950s

The history of redistricting in the area that is now Wisconsin goes back to 1787. I learned this from a 2020 document from the Wisconsin Legislative Reference Bureau, which provides a great service to all of us.

Our area was organized under the Northwest Ordinance into a territory in 1787. Representatives to the Territorial Legislature were elected from counties or townships. The Northwest Ordinance stated that inhabitants of the territory were entitled to "a proportionate representation in the legislature." As you read, you may conclude that this was a kind of stopgap solution. After all, we did not even have a president until George Washington was elected in 1788, the year after the Northwest Ordinance made the above decisions.

The 24th United States Congress created the Wisconsin Territory in 1836 when it created the Territorial Government of Wisconsin. This area included the now states of Wisconsin, Iowa, Minnesota, and parts of the Dakotas. This legislation gave the governor the power of legislative reapportionment. This struck me, and maybe you, that sole power being given to the executive feels like the way kings and queens in England controlled things. Democracy was still in the early stages.

The 1846 Wisconsin Territorial Convention was established to prepare Wisconsin for statehood, which occurred in 1848.

In Chapter 7, I discuss speaking in different communities in Wisconsin with former state Senator Dale Schultz about the issue of gerrymandering. We spoke in each other's districts, and while we were in Dale's district for a day, we visited Belmont and the site of Wisconsin's first capital, established there in 1836. It was temporarily moved to Burlington, Iowa, between 1837 and 1838 until the construction of the capitol building in Madison was finished in 1838. It would be the territorial capital because it would be ten more years in 1848 when we would become a state. Madison is the site of our current capitol building, although it has, of course, been rebuilt and modernized a few times before becoming the beautiful building it is now.

Our Belmont visit was very meaningful. It reminded me that Wisconsin started out growing in the southwest and had political clout in the Wisconsin Territory, or the capital would not have been in Belmont.

Part two of the Legislative Reference Bureau document traces the history of redistricting in Wisconsin and shows how the law and the process governing redistricting has evolved through at least three distinct eras over more than 200 years.

The first era was the Wisconsin Territorial era from 1787 until 1848, when Wisconsin became a state.

The second era was from 1848 until the 1960s. The state constitution required the legislature, not the governor, to draw the maps, and it required the legislature to reapportion every five years. Wisconsin had a census that showed the population change after five years. The census then changed to every ten years in 1910.

The third era lasted from the 1960s through today and into the future. This is the era of one person, one vote, due to a United States Supreme Court decision (see *Baker v. Carr*, 1962 in Appendix). So legislative and congressional districts must be reapportioned every ten years. If the legislature and the governor could not agree, the courts could and always have, in this situation, settled the new maps.

We do not know what the next era will look like and what will cause it. My speculation is that the adoption of a nonpartisan, Iowa-type system for redrawing maps could create the beginning of a new era. Some type of nonpartisan commission could conceivably work, but an Iowa-type system is my preference. I believe giving this issue to the federal courts would also work. I explain all this in detail in Chapter 9.

If you think politics is wild today, then let me take you back to the 1840s and 1850s.

- January 7, 1856: Because of a dispute over the 1855 gubernatorial election, both of the candidates in that election were sworn in as governor in separate ceremonies. The Democrat was incumbent William Barstow, and the Republican challenger was Coles Bashford.
- January 15, 1856: Assemblyman William Brunquest from northeast Wisconsin resigned his seat because it was demonstrated that he had actually lost his election.
- March 24, 1856: Governor Barstow withdrew his claim to the governorship, leaving Lieutenant Governor Arthur MacArthur Sr. as governor (those positions were not on the same ticket then).
- March 24, 1856: The Wisconsin Supreme Court ruled that Coles Bashford was the governor. So from January 7 to March 21, the people were not sure who was governor. This could be an entire book.

- While Wisconsin was still a territory, the power to draw the maps was given to the territorial governor with no legislative input. However, our first constitutional convention in 1846 enacted the power to reapportion only to the legislature.

- There was much disagreement as to whether there would be more than one legislator representing a district or just one!

Coles Bashford (above), William Barstow (at right). Photo credit for Bashford: Library of Congress Prints and Photographs Division. Brady-Handy Photograph Collection. Photo credit for Barstow: portrait by William F. Cogswell

- The 1846 proposed constitution was rejected by the voters in 1847. There were 14,199 votes for it and 30,231 votes against it.[16] These numbers are a reminder that the Wisconsin Territory was still not heavily populated.

The legislative districts in the 1840s under the new constitution did not come close to having equal populations in 1847. The ideal assembly seat should have had 3,290 people, but the largest district

had 6,487.[17] There were similar disparities for the state senate. These disparities were largely created by the framers of the constitution's choice to strictly adhere to county lines when drawing senate and assembly districts. Keeping counties intact had a partisan purpose. This is an example of where the word gerrymandering is not actually used but likely was the purpose behind the actions. It also likely shows the political power of county leaders in that era.

The total number of assembly and senate seats also changed. Wisconsin did not get to the current 33 senate seats and 99 assembly seats until 1972.

In 1892, the first major court battle over redistricting in Wisconsin—known as the "Cunningham cases"—would impact redistricting for decades. The state supreme court outlawed gerrymandering and said the court had the power to declare a reapportionment map unconstitutional.[18] This was 70 years before the U.S. Supreme Court made the same determination in *Baker v. Carr*.[19]

The Cunningham cases also established the one-person, one-vote rule decades before the U.S. Supreme Court did, although the rule was widely ignored for decades.[20]

I found it amazing that the Wisconsin Supreme Court, in the Cunningham cases, said that violating equal population "destroys one of the highest and most sacred rights and privileges of the people of this state, and that is 'equal representation in the legislature.'"[21]

However, after using this powerful language, including "sacred rights" of the people, the court opened the door to two exceptions. One exception was the right to keep counties intact. This made it more important to keep counties intact even if that map would not maintain a "sacred right." The bottom line is if equal populations in each district clashed with keeping counties intact, the idea of one person, one vote was put aside. So much for a sacred right.

The 1931 legislature passed a redistricting plan that underrepresented the more populous counties while overrepresenting the less populous counties. Since urban counties were more Democratic or Progressive and rural counties were more Republican, this felt like gerrymandering—and a legislature controlled by Republicans did it.

A classic example is that Milwaukee County, based on its population, should have had 24 or 25 assembly seats. Its population was about 25 percent of the state's population. The map gave them only 20 seats. However, Door and Kewaunee Counties, which were adjacent to each other, had a combined population equal to 1.17 percent of the state's population and, therefore, should have had one assembly seat. They were each awarded an assembly seat! Again, it feels like gerrymandering.

The map was challenged in the Wisconsin Supreme Court (see *Bowman v. Dammann*, 1932, in Appendix). The court refused to overturn the maps.

I will again say that when a court or a legislature decides on a map, look at the political results and ignore the explanation/defense.

The court also took the position that there is a "presumption of constitutionality," even if the map is a gerrymander.

What this means to me is that a gerrymandered legislative map challenged in the Wisconsin Supreme Court is presumed to be constitutional. This is a reason why I repeatedly say that if a solution to gerrymandering is to have the courts do it, then it should be the federal courts and not the state supreme court.

There was a "first" in the 1931 Bowman case. It was the first time I found the Wisconsin Supreme Court using the word *gerrymander* in their decision. The court said that the 1892 Cunningham cases had found that the maps being considered contained "clear and obvious gerrymanders."[22]

Yet the 1931 maps stayed in place.

I would like to write more about gerrymandering in those early years of statehood, but the word *gerrymandering* was almost never used. Early documents describe how all the legal requirements were met or not met, but the word *gerrymandering* is nowhere to be seen. Phrases I've seen used that might actually mean gerrymandering include "the maps did not appear to have a significant partisan implication" and "the districts were not properly contiguous, compact, nor convenient." And how would someone determine what is and isn't "convenient"?

The state supreme court in 1892 used the word *convenient*. I point this out because Wisconsin courts up to 2024 say that they never use the word *gerrymander* because there is no legal definition. Well, what is the legal definition of convenient? So the maps were not convenient. My dictionary's definition is "adding to one's comfort, causing little trouble or work, handy."

The 1931 legislature passed a plan that altered assembly district boundaries within counties without reapportioning seats. Therefore, more populous counties were underrepresented by the map, while less populous counties were overrepresented. This map looks, feels, and smells like a gerrymander, but of course, the word itself is never mentioned.

No congressional redistricting followed the 1940 census, although there were some minor revisions in 1943 and 1945. A petition was filed with the state supreme court asking the court to compel the legislature to try to redistrict. The court said it lacked that power. The court also said it "lacked the authority" to put a redistricting plan in place (this is different from the Wisconsin Supreme Court actions in 2022 and 2023).

This position that the court lacked the authority to redistrict was reversed in 1964.

Were you struck as I was that the state supreme court "lacked the authority" to put a plan in place? It seems that it "lacks the authority" unless it wants to and finds a reason why they have the authority.

There was some progress in the 1950s. The best-known effort was the Rosenberry Commission, led by the recently retired state supreme court Chief Justice Marvin B. Rosenberry.

The big issue was that Republicans were responding to their rural supporters who wanted the map drawing to consider not only population but also land. Including land areas as a factor would obviously lead to more political power than just using population. I admit I do not understand exactly how you would use land and population. Land has never been used as a factor.

This all led to statewide referendums and six court cases. The Rosenberry maps ended up being in place from 1954 through the 1962 election. These maps, considering only population and not land areas, led to Democrats gaining seats in the state legislature. The Rosenberry Commission's efforts ended, and all subsequent efforts at redistricting reform faced an uphill battle.

Redistricting reform efforts in Wisconsin have gone back more than 100 years. That none of those efforts have ever succeeded for as long as eight years tells us how difficult it is. My observation is that when you try to take power away from the powerful, they don't like it.

I have concentrated mostly on legislative map drawing, but I need to point out that between 1910 and 1960, congressional maps were only redrawn if the number of congressional seats in Wisconsin changed. This resulted in these maps allowing congressional districts to have different populations. This, of course, was sure to happen if the maps were only redrawn every 20 or 30 years.

My conclusion is that incumbent congressmen did not mind this process.

The year 1950 saw that a full redistricting plan of congressional seats had not been adopted in 30 years. There were just minor changes to the maps in 1931, and there were no changes following the 1940 census. This situation did not apply to legislative redistricting.

I felt it would be worth addressing what has happened to the size of our congressional delegation. It peaked at 11 congressional seats following the 1920 census and then decreased by one seat in each of the following census years, 1930, 1970, and 2000, and has stayed at eight since then. This means that the nation as a whole grew faster in population than in Wisconsin. Staying at eight means that Wisconsin's population has grown at about the same speed as the nation since 2000. Wisconsin's congressional delegation started at three with statehood in 1848 to the above-mentioned 11 following the 1920 census before declining to eight.

I could not find information that makes explicitly clear whether a partisan gerrymander occurred immediately after the 1950 census or any previous decades. My strong suspicion is that this is because no legislators ever want to restrain themselves. This, I suspect, would have happened whenever one party had total control of state government. There is good information in the Legislative Reference Bureau document, but it does not focus on the issue of gerrymandering. It focuses on legal issues such as equal population, the issue of keeping counties intact (a huge issue going back to the 1800s), compactness, contiguity, communities of interest, minority protection, competitiveness, and other requirements where you could improve, but the bottom line is that you could comply on all of the above issues and still gerrymander. Gerrymandering is very devious.

My conclusion after reading reapportionment accounts from the 1860s through the 1950s is that it "looks" like a lot of gerrymandering. Still, the word is very seldom used by historians and almost never by the state courts who decided on the issue.

The overriding importance that "keeping counties intact" had for decades feels like a gerrymander. Courts actually said that this was a higher level of importance than having as near as possible equal populations in each legislative district (1892 Cunningham cases).[23]

Just for fun, below are other interesting points about how legislative districts operated during the early years of Wisconsin's statehood:

- During the 1836–1848 Territorial period, there were "election districts." This meant that a legislative district could have more than one legislator serving that district.

- Members of the state assembly were elected for a term of one year and state senators for two years.

- There was a state census every five years. Therefore, reapportionment was every five years. Who thought that was needed?

- The most important thing that was never violated was the language that required counties to be intact.

[16] Michael Gallagher, Joseph Kreye, and Staci Duros, PhD. *Redistricting in Wisconsin 2020: The LRB Guidebook,* Wisconsin Legislative Reference Bureau, Wisconsin Elections Project, vol.1, no. 2, 2020, 38, https://docs.legis.wisconsin.gov/misc/lrb/wisconsin_elections_project/redistricting_wisconsin_2020_1_2.pdf.

[17] Ibid., 39.

[18] *The State ex rel. Attorney General v. Cunningham* 81 Wis. 440 (1892), https://www.wicourts.gov/courts/supreme/docs/famouscases12.pdf.

[19] *Baker v. Carr* (1962), Legal Information Institute, https://www.law.cornell.edu/wex/baker_v_carr_(1962).

[20] *The State ex rel. Attorney General v. Cunningham* 81 Wis. 440 (1892), https://www.wicourts.gov/courts/supreme/docs/famouscases12.pdf.

[21] Ibid., 5.

[22] Ibid.

[23] Ibid.

CHAPTER 4
Reapportionment Since the 1960 Census: Redistricting in the Era of One Person, One Vote

Why is 1960 to the present such an important time frame to address? I would call it "modern redistricting."

The 1960s saw some U.S. Supreme Court decisions that impacted redistricting after the court had refused to wade into this issue prior to the 1960s. The decade had this:

- Several decisions interpreted the 14th Amendment to the U.S. Constitution as requiring districts to be equal in population.

- *Baker v. Carr* (1962) saw the willingness of federal courts to weigh in on state legislative districts and impose remedies.[24]

- Equal population in each district had come to be viewed as a matter of justice.

- Technological advances allowed the U.S. Census Bureau to use computers for the 1960 census.

- Protection for racial minorities became a big federal issue in the 1960s and led to more attention being paid to the process of drawing district lines.

1961

The Republicans controlled the Wisconsin Legislature, and the governor was Democrat Gaylord Nelson. The legislature and governor could not agree on maps. However, on March 26, 1962, the U.S. Supreme Court issued its decision in *Baker v. Carr*, holding that federal courts could intervene in reapportionment matters.[25]

A huge issue from that time does not exist today. The legislative districts had nowhere near equal populations in the assembly or the senate. Assembly districts varied in population between 19,000 and 87,000. The senate district populations varied from 74,000 to 208,000. This outrageous situation existed because the "Cunningham cases" of 1892 declared that all counties must remain intact.[26] The 1890 elections saw a shift from Republican control of state government. Democrat George W. Peck was elected governor, and Democrats won significant control of both houses. Then came the Cunningham cases. My guess is this hurt Democrats in large-population counties and helped Republicans in smaller-population counties. The result of this is that Milwaukee and Dane Counties had more than one legislative seat but fewer seats than they would have had if the population was closer to equal in each district. The highest population of minorities was, no surprise, in Milwaukee County. This meant more assembly and state senate seats in more Republican areas of the state.

There were other legislative and judicial efforts, but the bottom line is that the 1962 elections were held under the existing maps.

This was understandable because the Republicans had control of both houses of the legislature with the existing maps, so I presume they were fine not reaching an agreement with the Democratic governor, which might not be as favorable to them as the existing ones.

The same disagreements between the Republican majority in the legislature and the Democratic governor, John Reynolds, carried over into 1963.

Finally, on May 14, 1964, the Wisconsin Supreme Court released its maps drafted by the court with the assistance of the nonpartisan legislative council. This was the first time in Wisconsin history that a court put in place a legislative redistricting plan. These maps would be used for the 1964 election. It is interesting to note that the 2024 maps were required to be in place by March 15, two months earlier than 1964. Sixty years later, we do have faster technology. However, I must acknowledge that in 1964, the primary was late (in September). Today it is one month earlier (in August), but still.

The court's maps made progress on population equity but were far from the perfection required in 2023.

The court's maps would also be the last time counties could not be split up. Wisconsin would have to wait until the 1970s to get maps that met the one-person, one-vote requirement of the 1962 *Baker v. Carr* decision. This was done by a court, and the 1970s would see the legislature abide by the *Baker v. Carr* decision.[27]

The 1964 election results occurred in a nationally big Democrat year. President Lyndon Johnson was elected to a full term after filling out the term of assassinated President John F. Kennedy. In Wisconsin, Republican candidate for governor Warren Knowles was elected to what then was a two-year term despite the big Democratic victory by Johnson. Knowles, who I got to know years later, was a smart, likable man who was moderate in his views. Democrat Patrick J. Lucey was elected lieutenant governor. You may be asking, "How could that be? Don't the governor and lieutenant governor run together on the ballot?" Not then. Wisconsin changed to that system in 1970 when we also switched from two-year terms to the four-year gubernatorial terms we have today. Knowles's popularity is shown by his being re-elected in 1966 and 1968 and then retiring and not seeking a fourth term in 1970.

The 1963–1964 session of the legislature had 20 Republicans, 10 Democrats, and 3 vacancies in the state senate. The Republicans had 20 state senate seats after the election, and the Democrats had 13. It is necessary to point out that only 17 of the 33 state senate seats were up for re-election, as the other 16 were at the midpoint of their four-year term.

The Republicans also had the majority in the state assembly during that session with a 53–47 margin. The 1964 election saw the Democrats take control of the assembly 51–49.

Two huge national events occurred during that session in 1963. Martin Luther King Jr. delivered his "I Have a Dream" speech on the steps of the Lincoln Memorial on August 28, and President Kennedy was assassinated in Dallas, Texas, on November 22.

The top-of-the-ticket election results showed the national results to be a Democratic landslide, as President Johnson won the election with 61.4 percent of the vote. Republican candidate Senator Barry Goldwater got 38.5 percent of the vote nationwide. Johnson won Wisconsin by a large margin. Democrat William Proxmire was elected U.S. senator.

Wisconsin voters showed they were willing to vote for the candidate of their choice regardless of party. This is partly why we have been called a "purple" state for the past several years.

1970

In 1972, the legislature drew the legislative maps. That decade, the Republicans controlled the senate, and the Democrats controlled the assembly and governorship.

The Cunningham cases of 1892 contained the "counties intact" requirement.[28] This one court decision greatly helps explain why the Republicans controlled the state senate from 1893 until the Democratic landslide of 1974. The 1972 reapportionment eliminated the Cunningham "counties intact" rule and was also an almost unheard of (and almost unrecognizable) agreement.

The legislature could not reach an agreement on their maps during 1971. Governor Lucey called a special session on April 19, 1972. The legislature agreed on maps, and it became law with Governor Lucey's signature on May 8, 1972. The agreement was a "bipartisan gerrymander."

This relatively brief description of the 1970s reapportionment does not include the politics behind how the agreement was possibly reached.

The explanation for the 1972 bipartisan gerrymander is beyond its implications at that time as it reminds us of how different politics were 50 years ago compared to the almost complete inability of the political parties to work together on almost anything today.

The 1972 bipartisan gerrymander made some changes. One was that the current system of three assembly seats within each state senate seat was established. Many of you who have only known this structure couldn't know that over the previous 150 years, there were many different requirements. For example, parts of counties could not be in different districts, which, of course, led to many other consequences. Legislative districts were nowhere near equal population.

The new Democratic governor, Pat Lucey, believed he could work with Republicans on some big issues (and he did). So with a deadlock in the agreement on legislative maps, Lucey proposed a remarkable solution. He suggested that the Republican majority in the state senate draw their maps and that the Democratic majority in the state assembly draw theirs. Something else happened—we got a bipartisan gerrymander. The senate Republicans gerrymandered the state senate seats, and the Democratic representatives gerrymandered the state assembly seats.

This is my "exhibit one" for the point I made earlier that gerrymandering is not a partisan issue. It is a power issue. If legislators have the power, they will abuse it.

The first election held under these new maps was in 1974, and I will address what happened in the next chapter. I will say now that the only way for the minority party to overcome the majority party gerrymander was if there was a huge wave election for the minority party at the top of the ticket, and this impacts the legislative election as well.

1980

In 1981, federal judges drew the maps as Wisconsin again had a divided government.

The governor was Republican Lee Sherman Dreyfus. Democrats controlled the legislature. That was the first reapportionment year that I was in the state senate. I did not have a leadership role in this process.

The legislature passed, and the governor signed the congressional map with little controversy. Congressional redistricting and the politics around it deserve an explanation. It was simple.

Republican and Democratic congressmen would oversee the map drawing, reach an agreement, and then "tell the legislators to pass it without change." The legislature passed their maps. The politics behind it were pretty simple. The maps were drawn in compliance with the one-person, one-vote requirement, and counties were not kept intact. Each leader could pick one member to be helped with some gerrymandering. So the goal was simply to make an incumbent congressman safer by helping the two most in need of help. Put simply, this was a limited bipartisan gerrymander.

The above process was used through 2001. It was politically easy for the legislature to do what the congressional leaders wanted.

Passing their maps quickly and with no real debate pleased everyone (except the tax-paying voters if they knew it happened).

A panel of three federal judges drew the legislative map for the 1982 election, and it was conducted with this map. As an aside, the discussion surrounding the map did not include the issue of gerrymandering. They discussed a more equal number of citizens in each assembly and senate district and tried to keep communities as intact as possible. Unspoken in public was how or whether the maps helped Democrats or Republicans more.

The 1982 elections under this new map kept a Democratic majority in each house. A Democrat, Tony Earl, was elected governor. Governor Dreyfus had not sought re-election. It is worth stating again that if the maps are "fair," then the party that won the top statewide race (in 1982, that was the governor's race won by a Democrat) would likely win more legislative races. They did in 1982.

The Legislative Reference Bureau stated, "Although, in the 1980 cycle, the legislature ended up enacting a plan that superseded but did not deviate substantially from the court's plan."[29] The best evidence that this was not a gerrymander is that in the first election run under this plan, the Democratic majority in the state assembly lost seven seats in 1984. If that was a gerrymander, it was the most incompetent one in gerrymander history!

1990

In 1991, the government was again divided as Democrats controlled both houses, and Republican Tommy Thompson was governor. That year the legislature and governor couldn't agree on maps, so a federal three-judge panel drew them. The panel's plan took effect on June 2, 1992, and the 1992 election took place under that map. Interestingly, a plan that took effect on June 2 was still enough time to have the maps apply to the 1992 elections, but in 2024, the deadline was March 15. Even taking into account that the primary had been moved up to August from September still makes this very interesting!

The federal judges, of course, drew "fair maps."

After much deliberation over four different plans (maps) drawn by the legislature, the court decided to draw their own and consider the "best" attributes of two of the plans.

2000

In 2001, the government was again divided, with Democrats controlling the senate and Republicans controlling the assembly and governor's office. That year Wisconsin's congressional seats were reduced from nine to eight. (Wisconsin's population grew in those previous ten years but not as quickly as other states, so we lost a seat.) Federal judges again drew the congressional maps, and again, it was no surprise that there was no gerrymander. The legislature passed the map, and Governor Scott McCallum signed it.

The legislative districts were another matter. The federal court rejected a proposed Republican map and a proposed Democratic map because of their "partisan origins." These maps were a Republican and Democratic gerrymander, though the "G" word was not actually used.

The federal judges said all of the maps suggested to them—there were more maps than the above two—had "unredeemable flaws." (Their term for gerrymandering?) The federal judges drew their own maps, which were used in the 2002 elections.

In all the decades discussed in the Legislative Reference Bureau from 1960 through 2020, it jumped out at me that the courts and the parties that filed maps for the courts to consider stated almost 100 percent of the time that their maps improved on all the "legal requirements," such as equal population in each legislative district, treating large minority population districts fairly, keeping municipalities intact as much as possible, "blah, blah, blah." *Everyone* involved in the process knew that the overwhelming issue was the maps were drawn to help one party—gerrymandering.

The word *gerrymandering* would never be mentioned. It was like it was one of those words that, if used when you were young and your mother heard it, would lead to you getting your mouth washed out with soap.

2010

In 2011, gerrymandered maps were drawn by the legislature as Republicans had won control of all branches of state government in the 2010 elections. I discuss this in Chapter 6.

I discuss these previous decades to point out that in 2011, Wisconsin had not had a partisan gerrymander since at least the early 1950s. I am 80 years old now. I was six years old in 1950. A very small percentage of today's population was at least 15 years old in 1950. I use this age and not the legal voting age of 21 then because many students this age are interested in government. To be 15 in 1950 would make you 89 years old today. The people of Wisconsin had no experience or knowledge of what gerrymandering meant for state government and how their voices could be silenced when the Republicans dropped gerrymandered maps on Wisconsin in 2011.

24 *Baker v. Carr* (1962), Legal Information Institute, https://www.law.cornell.edu/wex/baker_v_carr_(1962).

25 Ibid.

26 *The State ex rel. Attorney General v. Cunningham* 81 Wis. 440 (1892), https://www.wicourts.gov/courts/supreme/docs/famouscases12.pdf.

27 *Baker v. Carr* (1962), Legal Information Institute, https://www.law.cornell.edu/wex/baker_v_carr_(1962).

28 *The State ex rel. Attorney General v. Cunningham* 81 Wis. 440 (1892), https://www.wicourts.gov/courts/supreme/docs/famouscases12.pdf.

29 Michael Gallagher, Joseph Kreye, and Staci Duros, PhD. *Redistricting in Wisconsin 2020: The LRB Guidebook*, Wisconsin Legislative Reference Bureau, Wisconsin Elections Project, vol.1, no. 2, 2020, 22, https://docs.legis.wisconsin.gov/misc/lrb/wisconsin_elections_project/redistricting_wisconsin_2020_1_2.pdf.

CHAPTER 5

1974 and 1978: Running for the State Senate in a District Gerrymandered Against My Party

I've noted there was no widespread partisan gerrymandering in Wisconsin from the 1950s to 2011, but I confronted the bipartisan gerrymander that had occurred in 1972 when I ran for state senate in the 15th District in 1974. I was working on the staff of U.S. Representative Les Aspin (later U.S. Secretary of Defense) at the time. The bipartisan gerrymander two years earlier had given a large advantage to the district's incumbent Republican senator, James D. Swan of Elkhorn.

For decades the district had been made up of Rock and Walworth Counties on the state line, south of Madison. The 1972 gerrymander took nearly all of the largest city, Janesville, out of the district except for one ward, which was, unsurprisingly, very Republican. Janesville was rapidly changing into a Democratic city, and it was my hometown. The rest of the district was the Democratic city of Beloit, eastern Rock County, almost all of Republican Walworth County, and western Racine County, which was also Republican. Previous top-of-the-ticket elections showed it to be a 58 percent Republican district.

You might be asking, would I run in a 58 percent Republican district without almost all of my hometown? Janesville was the largest city in the district. I would also be running against a seven-year incumbent. The answer is that I had a few things I believed would help me, and they did.

Watergate

Watergate was a huge national issue that engulfed Republican President Richard M. Nixon. He had been exposed in the senate hearings by the Watergate Committee to be lying to the American people about his role in the scandal, which involved a break-in at the Democratic National Committee headquarters in a building in Washington named the Watergate. The Watergate Committee hearings were covered almost daily on TV with huge audiences as the American people took a big interest in the issue. They were very well informed on the issue, and they voted on their conclusions in November 1974. The issue had led to Nixon resigning in disgrace that July (he otherwise would almost certainly be impeached), and in September his successor, Gerald R. Ford pardoned him. This infuriated the public even more. I, of course, did not know all of this when I entered the race in May, but I did know the Watergate scandals would likely make 1974 a Democratic year in the November elections.

The statewide elections in Wisconsin bore this out. Democratic Governor Patrick Lucey was re-elected to a second term by the margin of 53 percent to 46 percent (1 percent for "other"). While this is not a landslide, it was a solid victory for Lucey, who did not go into the election year with high popularity ratings. He was a really good governor and a strong one, but never broadly popular.

Democratic United States Senator Gaylord Nelson was seeking a third six-year term and won by a huge margin. Nelson's margin was more telling of the mood of Wisconsin voters that year.

I have written about the impact the Watergate scandal had on legislative elections in Wisconsin in 1974. It made me think about how many Americans today remember it.

I look at it this way: If you are 60 years old today, you were a child in 1974.

Watergate is slipping deeper into our nation's history.

I do, of course, completely acknowledge that many Americans have read about Watergate in class or on their own. This, I would say, is

Patrick Lucey Governor of Wisconsin from 1971–1977.
Photo credit: unknown author public domain

not the same as living through it as an adult. As an example of this, I was born in 1944 and have no personal remembrance of World War II but have learned about it.

My Job as Ombudsman for Congressman Les Aspin

Ombudsman is a Swedish word meaning "people's representative." I held office hours in every post office in Wisconsin's 1st Congressional District (Aspin's district), which included all of the post offices in the 15th State Senate District. These office hours were publicized in all the local newspapers and on local radio stations. People met with me and got to know me as someone who could help them with their problems with government (federal, state, and local), or they had opinions or issues they wanted me to convey to Aspin. I was not viewed as a political partisan. This ended up helping me in the many Republican areas of the district as well as in Beloit. Also, Aspin was popular, and this did not hurt me.

We Ran a Wonderful Grassroots Campaign

I promised to hold office hours in every post office if I won. This was not partisan, and it was a big deal. My opponent, when asked by the media if he would do the same, refused to commit to doing it.

Many volunteers knocked on doors for me, and I did this as well. There was no evidence my opponent did this.

We also made a big effort to get bumper stickers on vehicles—at high school football games, at shopping malls, or anywhere we heard crowds would be.

Money Was Not an Issue in the Campaign

Both Senator Swan's campaign and mine spent about $13,000. Adjusted for inflation, this would likely be $50,000 to $60,000 this year. That is almost nothing today, as we have had many state senate campaigns that have spent millions of dollars. Neither of us, obviously, used any television ads and not many radio ads either. We spent most of our money on yard signs, bumper stickers, and literature.

The campaign was going well, and then I benefited greatly from Nixon's resignation in July and the Ford pardon in September. National and state polling were pointing to a big Democrat victory in November.

Abortion was an issue in 1974, if only because the landmark *Roe v. Wade* decision had just been handed down by the United States Supreme Court in 1973. I do not recall it being an issue in my 1974 election campaign with Senator Swan. I never had a chance to talk with Swan as he had an illness in early 1975 and died that year. My guess is neither one of us wanted to make it an issue. Otherwise, it would have been one.

Election night 1974 came. Traditionally, Beloit votes were reported first. I felt I needed at least 65 percent of Beloit to have a chance to win. Beloit came in with 73 percent. (I love Beloit to this day.) This told me there was a decent chance we'd win. The rest of the evening we watched as the 73 percent lead dropped to 65, then 60, then 55, and then we won with 53 percent.

The big Democratic year helped three other Democratic candidates for the state senate Katie Morrison, Gary Goyke, and Tom Harnisch defeat Republican incumbents. We had won majority control of the state senate 18–15. But it takes a landslide top-of-the-ticket election to overcome a gerrymander. It happened.

I have said many times, kiddingly, that I never had a chance to thank Richard Nixon or Gerald Ford.

By 1974, the Democrats had not had the majority in the state senate since 1893. That's 81 years!

The year was also significant because Katie Morrison was elected to the state senate from the 17th District (southwest Wisconsin). Why was this significant? Katie was the first woman ever elected to the state senate. Yes. We became a state in 1848, and it took 126 years before a woman would sit in the state senate. Of course, women could not even vote across America until 1920, but even with this progress, it took 54 more years before Katie won.

Those who designed the current capitol in 1920 must have never expected a woman to serve in the state senate because there was, in 1974, a men's room just off the senate floor but no women's room anywhere near the senate. The rest of us in the senate had this rectified very quickly.

In 1978, I faced re-election with the same district lines as in 1974. The year 1978 was not good for Democrats. Democratic President Jimmy Carter was two years into his presidency. Those two years had not gone well for the U.S. The president always bears the brunt of the blame, and therefore, his party would not do well in the midterm 1978 elections.

I met President Carter in the spring of 1976 when he was running for president in the Wisconsin primary. I introduced him at a political rally in Janesville. I also was a delegate to the Democratic National Convention pledged to Carter. My stepson, Mark MacKinnis, was with me at that rally in Janesville, and he had a chance to meet, talk with, and shake hands with someone who would become president of the United States—a thrill for Mark and me.

My four-year term expired in 1978. The Republican gerrymander of the state senate was still in place. I was seeking re-election for a second term without the benefit of Watergate and ex-President Richard Nixon and ex-President Gerald Ford. Also, Democratic President Jimmy Carter was two years into his presidency, and his polling numbers were not good.

I knew I would have to win re-election in a district that was 58 percent Republican and 42 percent Democrat based on top-of-the-ticket results in the 15th District. I knew I would get no help this time from a Democratic wave.

I worked extremely hard on constituent services, helping people with their problems with the government (federal, state, and local). I held office hours in every post office in the district. I did this frequently on Mondays and Fridays (when we would not be in session in Madison). I also started to have telephone office hours. I would sit at a phone after we would notify newspapers, dailies, and weeklies (yes, there were many of those papers then) and radio stations (and there were more of these as well) of the times and the phone number. I would use a 608 area code number for Rock County and go to a friend's home in Elkhorn to use his 414 area code phone number so that almost everyone in the 15th Senate District could call me as a local call. (How times change. Any call outside your area code was long distance for the caller with a special charge for each call.) These calls were very popular. I would hang up from one call, and the phone would ring again. I would schedule those for two or three hours each. If it was a state matter, I would then contact the appropriate state agency, asking them to look into it. For federal issues, I would contact my former boss, Congressman Les Aspin's office. For local issues, I would contact the appropriate local government office.

I received a call in late 1978 that told me much about how big this effort had become. The Department of Health and Social Services Secretary, Donald Percy, called me. He had asked his staff which legislators they were contacted by. He thought I would want to know the results of the survey. He said of all the contacts they received from all 132 legislators, 25 percent came from my office. I was astounded by this number. But then I wondered why they didn't get more requests for help from other legislators?! It told me all these "office" and "telephone" office hours were working. I would send a letter or letters to the citizen who contacted me (with a copy of the letter I had sent to the proper department/office on their behalf) and follow up as necessary.

People would contact me regarding state issues or legislation I would be voting on. I would tell them my views and follow up with a letter or letters on the status of the issue in Madison.

My 1978 campaign was run with a great staff of really hardworking volunteers. The campaign was run with no TV costs, and almost all the money went for yard signs, bumper stickers, brochures, and radio and local newspaper ads. I do not know the total costs, but it was most $40,000. I believe it was less but do not want to mislead you.

Election night saw me re-elected with 58 percent of the vote! It was a happy night. Of course, I was not running against an incumbent (as in 1974), and my opponent, Casey Olson, did not run an expensive campaign.

What about the other state senators who won in the Democratic landslide of 1974? How did they do in 1978? Unfortunately, Katie Morrison lost her re-election to Richard Kruel. She could not overcome the heavy Republican tilt of her district, and Kruel was a good candidate. He was on a local school board and had a very likable personality.

Tom Harnisch and Gary Goyke both won re-election. Good people, and this likely shows the power of incumbency if you are also a good candidate. The bottom line is the Democrats kept their majority.

I shared my campaign story to show there is a way to survive a gerrymander. If you are an incumbent, do what I did. I must also admit that my experience as Les Aspin's ombudsman certainly helped. I had promised in the 1974 campaign that I would continue to have those office hours as their state senator. And I did.

Candidates fighting the gerrymandered maps can pray for a national or state "wave" in favor of their party like in 1974, or try what I did leading up to the 1978 re-election. Wear out some shoes and be exhausted at the end of each day from knocking on doors, meeting people on their doorstep, and telling them how hard you work for them through office hours.

CHAPTER 6

2011: The Year Gerrymandered Maps by One Party Came to Wisconsin and How It Relates to Act 10

I was elected to the state senate again in 2010, 24 years after I had left to join Governor Tommy Thompson's cabinet as Secretary of the Department of Health and Social Services, which then included the Corrections Department.

I was elected, but 2010 was a Republican year in Wisconsin. The top-of-the-ticket results (the governor's race that year) are almost always reflected in the results of the legislative races. They were in 2010. Republicans won the governor's race and both the state senate and the state assembly. The margins were not landslides but were solid. The 2010 elections were run with the maps drawn by the federal judges in 2001. Hence, no gerrymander.

Everything would change in 2011, however, as Republicans used their total control of state government to—you guessed it—gerrymander. Parties with complete control seemingly cannot resist this abuse of power.

Once again serving in the senate, I had a front-row seat to the Republican gerrymander of 2011.

First, some background.

The 2009–2010 Wisconsin state government had a Democratic governor and Democratic control of both houses. I and other former Democratic legislators urged them to enact a nonpartisan Iowa-type plan for drawing the legislative maps following the 2010 census. They refused to take this advice.

Why did they refuse? They would never say, but I believe I know. The reason was simple. Democrats believed they would still control state government after the 2010 election, allowing them to draw the new maps in 2011. They were disastrously mistaken. Democrats lost on all fronts, and Republicans drew the maps. What a lost opportunity. We could have ended gerrymandering in Wisconsin, as Iowa has now done for over 40 years. I am not saying this would have been easy to pass, but the Democrats did not even try.

Wisconsin voters have made an amazingly consistent decision when it comes to gubernatorial elections. Going back to 1964, no candidate of the same party as the outgoing governor has ever won. Wisconsin voters have not trusted the same party for long periods of time. The only exception was the four terms when they elected Tommy Thompson. Still, when Thompson left and his last term expired, the voters picked Democrat Jim Doyle in 2002.

Election Results:

1964 Republican Warren Knowles replaced Democrat John Reynolds

1970 Democrat Patrick Lucey replaced Republican Warren Knowles

1978 Republican Lee Dreyfus replaced Democrat Patrick Lucey

1982 Democrat Tony Earl replaced Republican Lee Dreyfus

1986 Republican Tommy Thompson replaced Democrat Tony Earl

2002 Democrat Jim Doyle replaced Republican Tommy Thompson

2010 Republican Scott Walker replaced Democrat Jim Doyle

2018 Democrat Tony Evers replaced Republican Scott Walker

I am talking about the party changes after an incumbent served one, two, or, in Governor Thompson's case, four terms, and this change occurred in elections, not when the incumbents resigned and then were replaced by their lieutenant governors who were in the same political party.

There have been two resignations by a governor since 1970. Governor Lucey resigned in 1977 to become ambassador to Mexico in the President Carter administration. Lieutenant Governor Martin Schreiber finished his term. Republican Lee Dreyfus won the next election. Governor Thompson resigned as governor in 2001 to become the Secretary of Health and Human Services in the President George W. Bush administration. Lieutenant Governor Scott McCallum finished his term. Democrat Jim Doyle won the next election.

Martin Schreiber Governor of Wisconsin 1977-1979.
Photo credit: Martin Schreiber and mytwoelaines.com

If the Democratic leadership in 2009–2010 had looked at this history, it could have made them unsure about the likely results of the 2010 governor's race, let alone the legislative results. They would obviously not know the 2010 and 2018 election results, but they should have known the pattern from 1964 to 2002.

In the 2010 election, the voters chose Republican Scott Walker to be their governor, and Republicans won control of both houses. We all know what happened next—a Republican gerrymander of both houses that lasted 13 years. How did that work out for the Democrats?

There is nothing wrong with hoping to keep power. A legislature certainly can pass more legislation they believe in if they are in the majority rather than the minority. But for any elected official who believes in democracy, aiming to keep power with the specific goal of gerrymandering should be called out.

The Republicans abused their power and drew maps that were a gerrymander. To paraphrase a famous statement: "Absolute power leads to absolute abuse of power," and that is what happened in 2011. Gerrymandering allows a party to control the legislature in years when the statewide voter mood is near 50–50 or when it is a modest-sized victory for the minority party. The victories by the majority party are not even close or competitive. A strong majority of gerrymandered districts are won by at least 60 percent to 40 percent.

The legislature and Governor Walker rushed through their gerrymandered maps so quickly that, for the first time, the maps were passed into law before the counties and municipalities could draw wards. This broke with state precedent.

This map led to a lawsuit that went to the U.S. Supreme Court (*Gill v. Whitford*).[30] The high court did not rule on the merits of the case but dismissed it because the plaintiffs "lacked standing."

The most significant gerrymander case to go to the U.S. Supreme Court was *Benisek v. Lamone* (see Appendix). This case dealt with a gerrymander in Maryland where the court stated that redistricting was a "political question" that the court "could not adjudicate."31 What a disgusting way for the court not to do its job. One could easily argue that many cases involve a political question. Just look at their recent ruling on the highly political case of *Roe v. Wade*.

I regard, and I believe many would agree, that the 2011 redistricting in Wisconsin is one of the most egregious partisan gerrymanders in the history of the country. Republicans have near supermajorities in the senate and assembly. The bias of the 2011 maps was

Wisconsin Governor Scott Walker who signed the 2011 gerrymandered maps into law. Photo credit: Gage Skidmore

clearly illustrated again in the 2018 fall election when Democrats won every statewide race and won 53 percent of the statewide legislative vote, yet only won 36 of the 99 assembly seats. That is not democracy.

Readers may be wondering or concerned about the connection between the gerrymandered maps of 2011 and Act 10.

While many people know about Act 10, I should note that this was the 2011 law passed by the Republican majority and signed by Governor Scott Walker, who proposed this legislation.

Act 10 took away almost all collective bargaining rights to most state and local employees who were represented by a union. Governor Walker excluded police and firefighters from the law. (I believe he did not want to irritate those workers and his "law and order" constituencies.)

So, how are the two matters related? Republican legislators in gerrymandered seats could vote for it and not worry about their vote affecting their getting re-elected. Act 10 was a controversial law that divided the state. Republicans voting against it ran a great risk of facing a primary and maybe losing that election. I believe that if the legislature had not been gerrymandered by the Republicans, it would have been far more difficult to get it passed by both houses.

Legislators had to work through thousands of protestors for about two months to get to their offices. This was not a pleasant experience if you supported Act 10. If you were against Act 10, you were treated like royalty by the protestors.

Governor Walker came to his office in the capitol through a secret entrance in the basement. A tunnel runs from the basement of a state office building about one block from the capitol. I believe several other Republicans took this route, too.

Act 10 was dropped on the people of Wisconsin with no warning, like a bomb. That is the word that Governor Walker actually used to describe what he was doing.

The higher level comparison between gerrymandering and Act 10 is that both can only be done and get passed if one party (in this situation, the Republicans) has total control of state government.

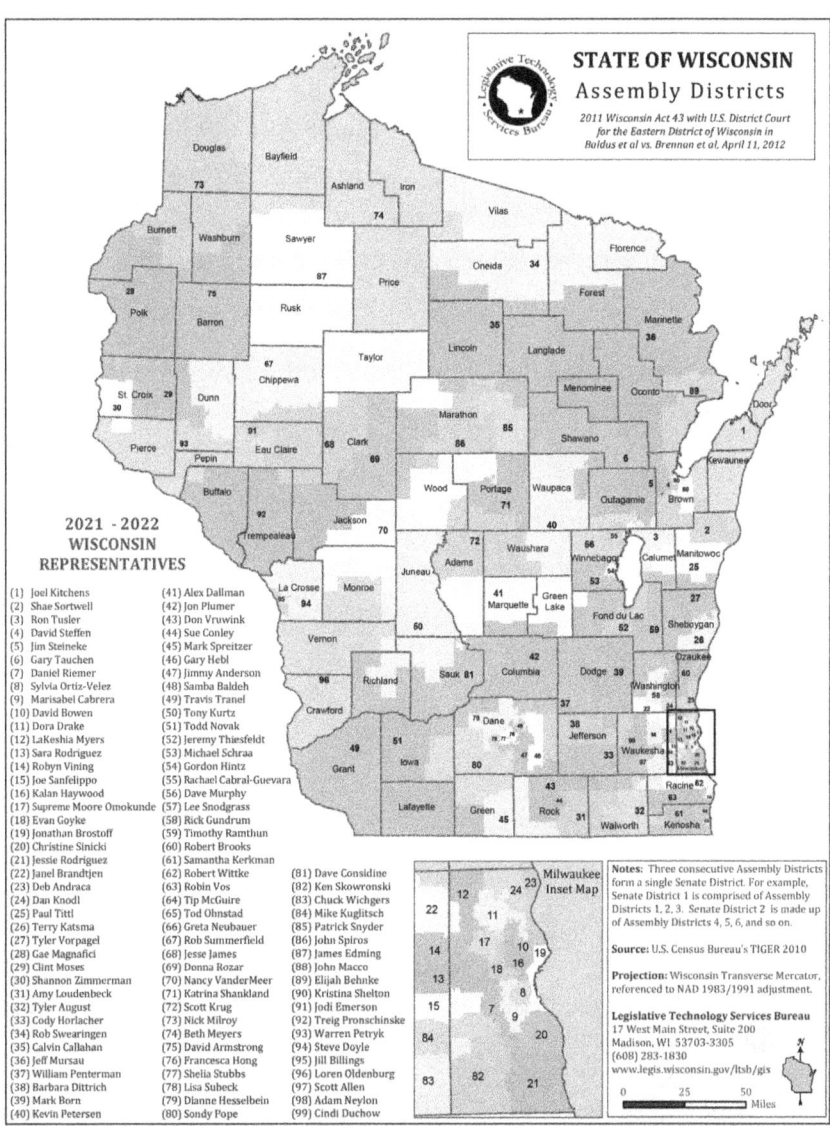

2011 Wisconsin Assembly District Map. Photo credit: Legislative Technology Services Bureau

WISCONSIN GERRYMANDERING 77

I use the Act 10 comparison, but the gerrymander also made voting for other of Governor Walker's controversial agenda items easier because the legislators represented "safe" districts and did not have to worry they may not be re-elected.

This also helps explain the speed at which the gerrymandered maps were drawn, introduced and passed, and signed by the governor. It also explains why Republican legislators were only shown their own district maps and not the rest of the state.

Why the speed? Because the sooner the gerrymandered maps were signed into law, the easier it would be to support Governor Walker's agenda and not worry about getting re-elected. Republicans also knew that if they still opposed some of Walker's legislative agendas, they could face a primary opponent who Walker may support.

I use Act 10 as an example. Other Walker legislative proposals were also controversial.

---

[30] "*Gill v. Whitford*," Brennan Center for Justice, July 3, 2019, https://www.brennancenter.org/our-work/court-cases/gill-v-whitford.

[31] "*Lamone v. Benisek*," Brennan Center for Justice, July 29, 2019, https://www.brennancenter.org/our-work/court-cases/lamone-v-benisek.

CHAPTER 7
Dale and Me

The Dale in the title of this chapter is former Republican state Senator Dale Schultz from Richland Center. We were in the Wisconsin State Senate together from 2011 to 2015.

We had always gotten along well but had not worked closely together until gerrymandering occurred in 2011. Dale and I first crossed paths in 2005 when he was chosen as the Republican state Senate Majority Leader. I had that job in the 1980s as a Democrat. I made an appointment with him in his office to talk about the job and what I had learned from it. Dale really appreciated that a Democrat was suggesting ways he could succeed in that job. We did not discuss any issues. I talked with him about process and dealing with your caucus, and so on.

We again connected in 2011 when I came back to the state senate, where Dale was still serving. So we had a good relationship when the gerrymander happened. Most important, we trusted each other.

I must acknowledge that there were people in the capitol in both parties who did not like our friendly relationship. I learned quickly how much things had changed since I was first there in the 1970s and early 1980s. Things had become highly partisan, and those across the aisle were to be regarded as the enemy.

Dale and I introduced the first legislation to adopt a nonpartisan Iowa-type redistricting plan for Wisconsin. It was no surprise, but that proposal was never allowed by the majority party to come to the floor of the state senate for a vote. It was not even given a public hearing.

Dale and I were sitting in the senate chamber one day when the senate was not in session, and the gerrymandered maps had just been passed and signed into law. It was the summer of 2011. Dale said something like, "What can we do?" We decided that we could go around the state together and deliver to the voters the message of the many bad consequences of gerrymandering. We let it be

Former State Senator Dale Schultz. Photo credit: Rachel Schultz

known that we would travel across Wisconsin together and speak to groups or organizations. The invitations came in. There was clearly interest in this issue. We did not keep track of our appearances, but between 2013 and 2019, we spoke at least 90 times.

We found (as we had expected) that because we were a Republican and a Democrat, and former majority leaders, groups like service clubs and the League of Women Voters were comfortable inviting us because they would not face criticism for inviting a member of just one party.

We brought with us three large legislative maps of Wisconsin, Illinois, and Iowa, showing a Republican gerrymander in Wisconsin, a Democrat gerrymander in Illinois, and a "fair map" from Iowa that the politicians did not draw. That old saying that "a picture is worth a thousand words" was very true with these maps.

A simplified way to look at these maps is to look for right angles in legislative districts. Wisconsin and Illinois have very few, and Iowa has a huge number of right angles. One glance tells all. There are no salamanders in the Iowa map.

Dale and I would talk about the issue and then take questions. During our first year or two, we would need to answer very basic questions. People asked, "Where did the word come from?" "Who was Elbridge Gerry?" "How does gerrymandering happen?" "What is the process?" "How are the maps drawn?" But in the later years, we didn't get these basic questions. We realized that the people of Wisconsin had learned a lot about gerrymandering, and they did not like it. To be clear, Dale and I were only partially responsible for this change. Several good government groups were doing their part. These groups included the League of Women Voters, Common Cause in Wisconsin, and the Wisconsin Democracy Campaign. The media certainly played a part by covering the issue.

I remember one night we were in Whitewater, and two things we heard that night jumped out at us. One man was there for gerrymandering and another cause he was supporting. He said after listening to us that he was going to have his group now be active against gerrymandering as well as the cause he was already supporting.

Also that night, a woman told us about meeting with her legislator to express her opposition to gerrymandering. She said in the give-and-take of their discussion, the legislator became irritated and told her, "You know, I didn't have to be here to talk with you!" The cold, sad truth is that with the legislator's gerrymandered district, he did not have to be there. He could say something like that and know that only the primary mattered. There was no way he could lose the general election. This legislator had nearly a 70 percent Republican district. Constituent relations can also take a hit from gerrymandering.

When Covid-19 happened in 2020, we suspended our efforts. By 2022, fortunately, both polling and advisory referendums in some 32 counties showed broad opposition to gerrymandering. These 32 counties included "red" counties and "blue" counties. Dale and I stopped touring.

Dale and I still talk by phone twice a month or more and occasionally speak on the issue when asked. We spoke in the capitol on November 21, 2023, when the state supreme court heard oral arguments on the lawsuit challenging the gerrymandered maps in Wisconsin. As I write this, our state has fair maps—finally.

We now have fair maps, perhaps until 2031, but we need to adopt an Iowa-type plan in Wisconsin soon. We may have a little over six years to get that done. But we for sure have one and a half years. Why do I say this? Because the Wisconsin Supreme Court election in the spring of 2025 could see a conservative elected and the fair maps endangered.

Justice Ann Walsh Bradley is one of the four justice majority who declared the legislative maps unconstitutional in December 2023. She had given some indication that she would run for re-election in 2025. This all changed on April 11, 2024, when Justice Bradley announced she would not run. Without an incumbent, that race may be close, and the fate of fair maps may hang in the balance.

Justice Bradley served with distinction for three ten-year terms and served in a time when the court was not the politicized body it has become. She did not refer to these changes in the court in her statement announcing that she would not run again. She did say she would be active on issues she cares about. She will still be making a difference.

I can't easily predict the outcome of the 2025 supreme court race. It will establish a 4–3 majority. A 4–3 conservative majority could take a lawsuit questioning the constitutionality of the maps that were in place for the 2024 elections. This may well be difficult because the current maps were passed by a Republican-controlled legislature and signed by a Democratic governor.

I can easily predict that the 2025 election will be a huge event with big money pouring in on behalf of the two candidates, and likely the most expensive supreme court race in Wisconsin history. Its importance and unpredictability only increased with Justice Bradley's announcement.

We must be ever vigilant and try to get the Iowa-type system in place by July 2025. The winning justice in 2025 will take their seat on the court in early August.

CHAPTER 8

February 19, 2024:
A Day to Celebrate—The People Won!

In November 2021, the Wisconsin Supreme Court, with a 4–3 conservative majority and the redistricting issue in front of them, declared that they would use the "least change" principle in deciding the maps for the 2022 election. Of course, this meant "least change" to the giant 2011 gerrymander drawn by the Republican legislature and signed by Republican Governor Scott Walker in 2011. The four conservative justices did this with a straight face and not giggling (at least not in public).

"Least change" to a gerrymandered map is gerrymandering without explicitly using the word. The justices can explain and explain why they don't use the word, but that doesn't mean that the public is at all fooled.

More recently, and again with straight faces, Republicans criticized Janet Protasiewicz, then a candidate in the state supreme court race, for just talking about gerrymandering during her campaign. You may have figured out that Protasiewicz was viewed as a "left-leaning" candidate.

"Least change" meant the obvious. We had just observed the effects of the 2011 gerrymander on legislative election results in 2012, 2014, 2016, 2018, and 2020. The results were huge Republican majorities irrespective of the voters' views, as seen by the top-of-the-ticket results for each of these years.

The court did alter the legislative district maps to adjust for population change over the previous ten years. They were required to do this (one-person, one-vote law), but these very modest changes did not disturb the gerrymander. This was clearly their private goal, but none of them would ever admit it. These four conservative justices knew exactly what they were doing. They were likely guaranteeing Republican control of both houses until at least 2032. Every reasonable person knew what their decision meant.

There is, of course, a strong precedent for state supreme courts and the United States Supreme Court to respect previous decisions on issues where these courts have decided the issue in the past. This is particularly true when the issue was decided decades earlier and became accepted in America.

"Least change" is a goal I largely agree with, but it is blatantly indefensible when it comes to using it to keep the 2011 Wisconsin gerrymander in place. "Least change" is a strong argument with the United States Supreme Court on considered "settled" law based on previous Supreme Court decisions. Maybe the state supreme court was actually claiming that a gerrymandered state legislative map is "settled indefinitely."

How can someone be sure gerrymandering is bad for democracy? One good way to measure is by looking at the difference between the results in 2022 with Republican maps in place and how the results would have differed had the 2024 maps been used.

The Republican maps for 2022 in the state senate races resulted in the Republican candidates winning control by a 22–11 majority. The 2024 maps signed by Governor Tony Evers would have resulted in a 17–16 Republican majority. Applying the same situation to the state assembly races in 2022 shows that the Republicans won a 60–39 majority. The Evers maps would have resulted in Republicans winning a 53–46 majority.

The closer margins are consistent with the top-of-the-ticket results in presidential elections as well as the U.S. Senate and races for governor. All have been close races for many elections, having been decided by margins as close as 50.5–49.5 percent. These statewide elections show how closely divided the state of Wisconsin is. The new maps will see their statewide voter views reflected in the state's legislative races.

The only way that the majority party could lose in 2024 with the 2021 maps in place is if there is an unprecedented wave election in favor of the minority party in the legislature and the Democrats are chosen by over 60 percent of the voters statewide. This is highly unlikely in a state where many statewide elections are decided on 51–49 percent or closer than that—a long way from 60 percent plus. This only happened once, in the state senate election of 1974.

On April 4, 2023, Janet Protasiewicz was elected to the state supreme court (perhaps an indicator of the views of the majority of Wisconsin voters on the issue of gerrymandering), changing the 4–3 conservative majority to a 4–3 liberal majority, and on January 29, 2024, Democratic Governor Tony Evers vetoed the Republican redistricting map (Assembly Bill 415). The veto was final, as the legislature did not override it.

That was important as it appeared the prospect of the legislature and governor reaching an agreement on a map was gone. The state supreme court had paused its involvement to see if there could be agreement between the legislature and the governor, but with no agreement, this would allow the court to move forward and put a redistricting map in place. They started that process. To most people's surprise, however, the Republican legislative leadership attached the original Evers bill (the bill mentioned above that he vetoed had been changed significantly) to another bill in what is called a "substitute amendment." This replaced the original bill. Have I confused this enough yet? Both houses, with overwhelming Republican support, passed the Evers legislation, and he signed it on February 19, 2024.

This means the people of Wisconsin will have fair maps for the 2024 elections. The maps were sent to the State Election Commission before the March 15 deadline. If new maps had not arrived at the commission by March 15, the 2024 legislative elections would have been run using the 2022 Republican gerrymandered maps. The new maps would not have been able to be used until 2026.

The 2024 elections will be the first non-gerrymandered state senate and assembly elections since 2010. The November 2024 general election of the state legislature will matter again.

There was huge opposition to the vote by legislative Democrats. They believed they could get even "fairer" maps if the state supreme court drew new maps. What's that old saying? "Don't let the 'perfect' get in the way of the good." I believe Governor Evers did the right thing by signing this legislation despite the Democratic opposition. His maps are fair, given the slight Republican tilt, which is due to where Democrats and Republicans live in Wisconsin.

The governor's maps put several incumbents in both houses into the same district. So their options are to run against each other, move their residence to their new district, or just retire. Some are in the same district with another legislator who belongs to the same party, hence a primary election would happen if they both ran. If they belong to different parties, they would face off in the November general election.

The incumbent pairings in the assembly total 15 pairs:

11 districts pair two Republicans

1 district pairs two Democrats

3 districts pair a Democrat and a Republican

The incumbent pairings in the senate total 6 pairs:

2 districts pair two incumbent Republicans

1 district pairs three incumbent Republicans

1 district pairs two incumbent Democrats

1 district pairs an incumbent Democrat and Republican

The incumbents affected by the above pairings and their supporters are very unhappy with these maps. Now, unless they move their residences, one of them (and two in one state senate seat because three are paired into one district) will not be in the legislature in 2025.

I understand incumbents affected can be unhappy. However, I think they should ask themselves how we arrived at this situation. The answer is that the 2011 and 2021 gerrymanders required a fair map to end those gerrymanders. Without those gerrymanders, they likely would not have enjoyed the job security they had for 14 years. Some of the legislators affected did not serve all 14 years. However, another legislator from their party served the other years.

The above information is from a report by Marquette University Law School Research Fellow John Johnson.

The people of our state have not won very often in the state capitol, but they won on February 19, 2024.

These maps will be in place until new maps are drawn following the 2030 census unless the state supreme court swings conservative and a lawsuit successfully challenges the 2024 maps.

This means we have six years—or conceivably less—to pass an Iowa-type nonpartisan process for drawing non-gerrymandered maps. The hope is those maps might stay in place in perpetuity. Why do I say "Iowa type" rather than "Iowa?" Because Wisconsin is not Iowa, and we should make sure our solution fits Wisconsin. Iowa does not have any city nearly as large as Milwaukee. It is also a far more rural state, so it is easier to draw maps with right angles (right angles are a huge indicator of no gerrymander). Additionally, Iowa gives the final say if maps are not agreed upon after three times to their supreme court. I do not think this is a good long-term solution in our state, with narrow judicial majorities that could change each year there is a state supreme court election. The goal needs to be that the state legislature cannot have the final say on the maps—period.

The Brennan Center for Justice reported the following information entitled, "What States Can Learn from Wisconsin's Win for Fair Maps." It was published on March 6, 2024. The piece was authored by Peter Miller.

The subtitle says it all: "The state ensured its new legislative district plan is both politically neutral and responsive to voters." What a worthy goal to have achieved.

There were 13 statewide contested elections from 2016 to 2022. The top-of-the-ticket results in those 13 races show that Democrats won 50.8 percent of the two-party vote. The best a Democratic candidate did was 55.4 percent received by Tammy Baldwin in the 2018 U.S. Senate race, and the worst was 48.3 percent received by Russ Feingold in the 2016 U.S. Senate race.

I believe the best illustration of the unfairness of the 2011 gerrymander, which was only slightly tweaked by the conservative majority of the Wisconsin Supreme Court in 2022, is to look at what share of the statewide vote the Republicans would need on the same election day to result in a near supermajority of both houses of the state legislature. The answer is they would need to get only 48 percent of the statewide vote.

The same day, the statewide vote for Republicans was 48 percent, but in a strong majority of state assembly and senate seats, they won by 60–40 or by a much larger margin. If you're pro-gerrymandering, Wisconsin certainly had a good one.

The Republicans actually came close to a supermajority in the assembly. Two-thirds is a supermajority, and they achieved it in the senate in 2022 with a 22–11 margin.

A supermajority in both houses means one really important thing. When they pass a bill the governor disapproves of, he can veto it, and that kills the bill, except if the legislature overrides his veto with a two-thirds vote in each house. An override means a bill becomes law in spite of the governor's veto. It neuters one of the governor's biggest powers. In Wisconsin, you can only accomplish supermajorities with a gerrymander. The governor's signing of the new maps bill (now called Act 94) ends this possibility as long as Act 94 maps stay in place until 2031 and then are either continued or replaced by new fair maps that may have been tweaked due to population change. We can't know whether either party will have total control of state government after the 2030 election.

Fair maps will not guarantee that most state assembly and senate districts will be competitive. Those of us who want non-gerrymandered districts should not expect this. Why? Because of where Republican and Democratic voters live. Fair maps will try to keep communities, including counties, cities, villages, and towns intact. The motive cannot be to create competitive districts by gerrymandering competition at the expense of dividing cities, villages, towns, and counties and running district lines down the middle of a street so you and your neighbor across the street are in different districts.

Fair maps could avoid creating competitive districts in Madison, Milwaukee, and several smaller cities that vote for Democrats by large margins. Likewise, some counties around Milwaukee on the west and north side and many rural counties are solidly Republican and should not have their communities of interest gerrymandered in the name of "competition."

Fair maps could lead to about 35 or so Democratic-leaning or strongly Democratic districts based on where Democratic voters live and about 35 or so Republican-leaning or strongly Republican districts based on where large percentages of Republicans live. That leaves about 30 districts very competitive districts, and things like whether it is likely going to be a Democratic or Republican year in the top-of-the-ticket races (governor, U.S. Senate, or presidential races) decide which party gets the most votes. Other factors include the quality of each candidate, who has the most effective campaign, and who raises the most money. Money, particularly from special interest groups, never sits out an election.

Before the Republican gerrymander of 2011, when federal judges drew the maps in Wisconsin in 1981, 1991, and 2001, this was about the breakdown of legislative districts and, no surprise, the party that won the election at the top of the tickets won or nearly won control of the two houses of the legislature. In no election in those 30 years did one party win the top-of-the-ticket race and lose 60 percent or more of the legislative races. It is, of course, no surprise that those federal judges did not draw gerrymandered maps.

There are big positives for democracy, with the legislature and governor agreeing on new maps. Replacing the gerrymandered map means that there is now little chance that the Republicans or Democrats can get a two-thirds majority and have the ability to override a gubernatorial veto. Supermajorities destroy our structure of state government, where the governor and legislature are co-equal branches of government. That is an insult to the voters of Wisconsin when this power to override a veto is possible only because of a gerrymandered map. People in Wisconsin know we are close to a 50–50 state at the top of the ticket, so this power can only be realized with a gerrymander. I must make clear that if, in a situation with fair maps, the voters elect two-thirds of both houses for a party different from the governor's, then the people have done this with their votes, and so be it. The people will have neutered the governor's power fair and square.

The recruitment of candidates will also change with no gerrymander. No longer will either party need to emphasize the ability of the candidate to win a primary, i.e., left-of-center Democrats and right-of-center Republicans. They now will recruit candidates who can win a general election in a competitive district.

I believe another important point is that non-gerrymandered legislators can be more politically safe to work with legislators in the other party to get something done. If they're perceived as moderate, it won't hurt and very likely will help them in the general election.

Another improvement will be that legislative leaders, while they still will have access and big influence with large donors and large political action committees, won't be likely to use that money against an incumbent in their own party in a primary. The leader will realize that for them to stay in the majority or gain the majority, they will need the more moderate legislators to win their legislative seats.

Even though eliminating gerrymandering doesn't guarantee 100 percent competitive districts, my easy conclusion from all of the above is that the people of Wisconsin, and democracy, are far better off.

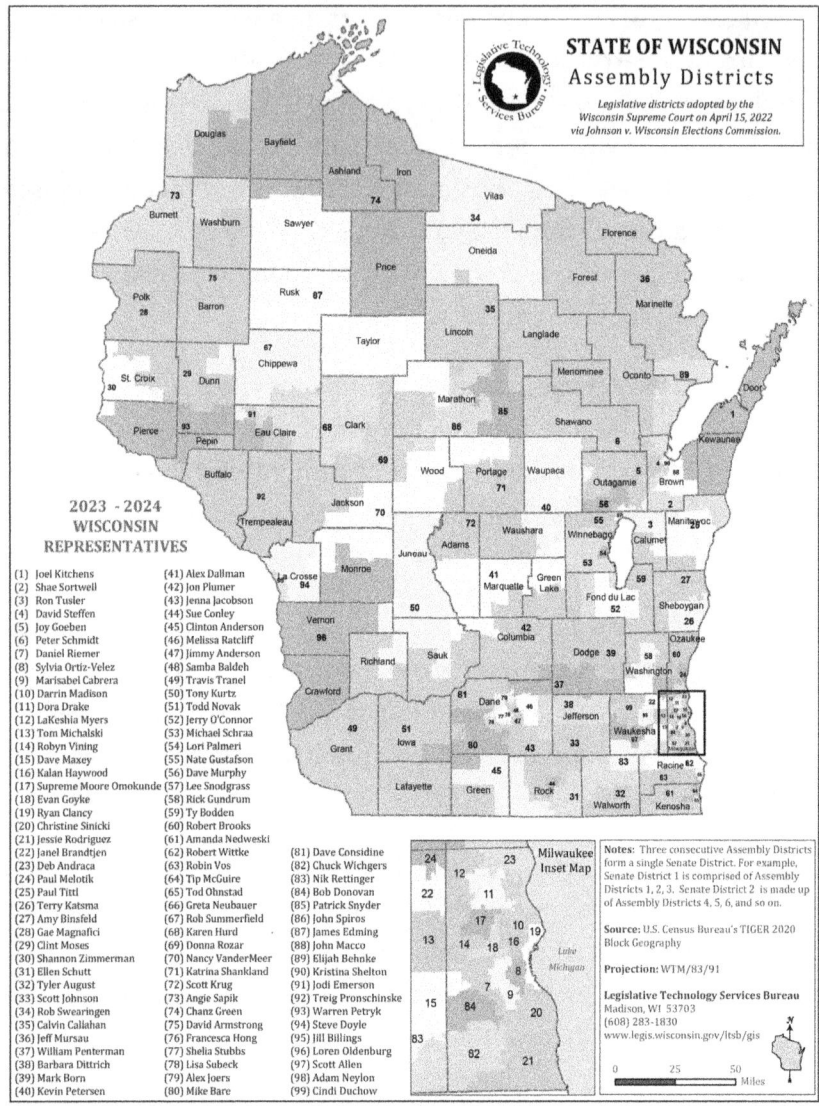

Republican gerrymandered state assembly map enacted in 2022 (above) and Assembly Districts 2024 redrawn map (right).
Photo credits: Legislative Technology Services Bureaua

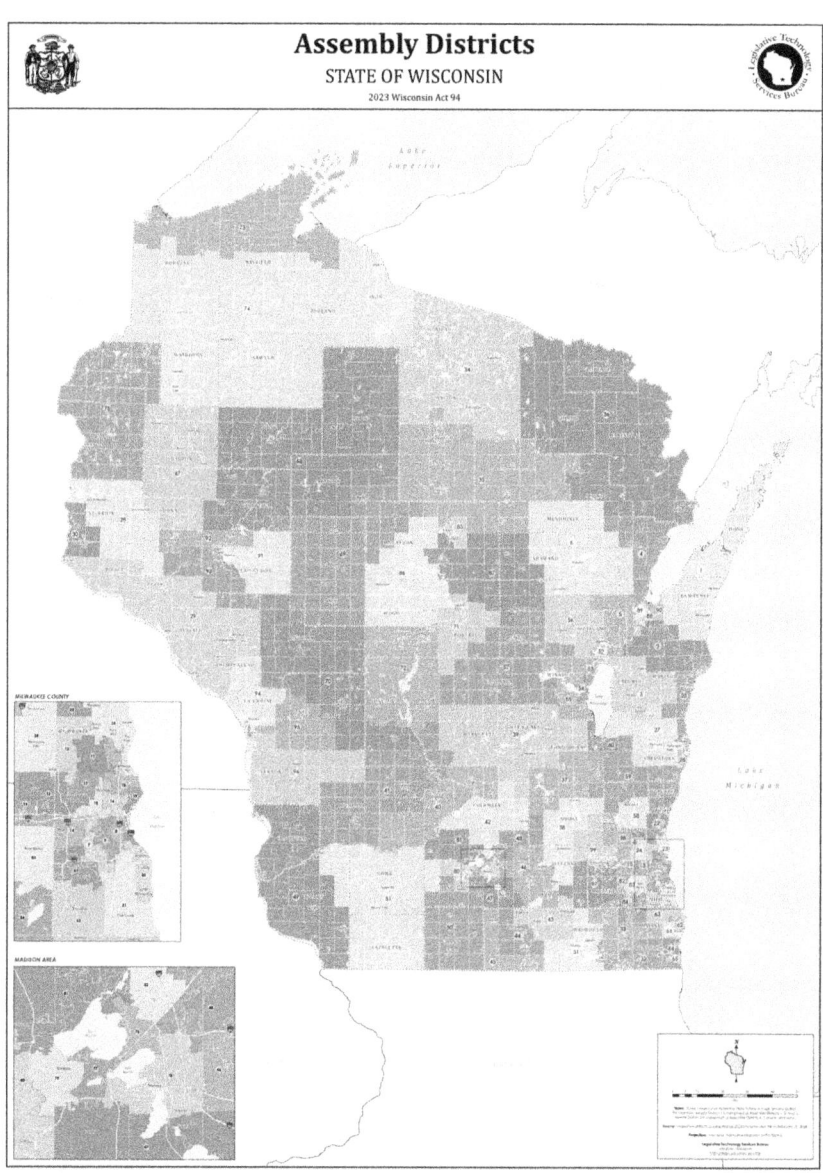

WISCONSIN GERRYMANDERING

CHAPTER 9
How to End Gerrymandering

How do the people of Wisconsin feel about gerrymandering? A January 2019 Marquette University Law School poll found that 72 percent of Wisconsin voters want to see redistricting done by a nonpartisan commission (the other 18 percent prefer redistricting stay in the hands of the legislature and governor).[32] Seventy-two percent means there is opposition across the political spectrum.

Groups, organizations, and partnerships were formed to fight the issue in the state. The Wisconsin Fair Maps Coalition started in 2017 for this purpose. The major groups in this coalition are Citizen Action of Wisconsin, Common Cause in Wisconsin, Wisconsin Fair Elections Project, League of Women Voters of Wisconsin, Wisconsin Democracy Campaign, and Wisconsin Voices. In Chapter 7, "Dale and Me," I tell of the efforts of former Republican state Senate Majority Leader Dale Schultz and me. We traveled around Wisconsin together between 2013 and 2019, speaking to groups from Racine to Superior and La Crosse to Milwaukee.

Since most Wisconsin voters are opposed to gerrymandering, they should demand answers from candidates on the gerrymandering issue. Do not be satisfied with the "complex" and "complicated" responses. Evasive answers could be avoided if there were an organized effort by pro-reform groups and the media asking all candidates for the state legislature to answer a simple question *before* the elections. "Will you vote for a solution that takes the process of reapportionment out of the control of the legislators?" This is a yes or no question.

The media would then need to be committed to widely publicizing the candidates' responses. Refusing to respond should be regarded as a "no." Pro-fair maps groups also could publicize these responses.

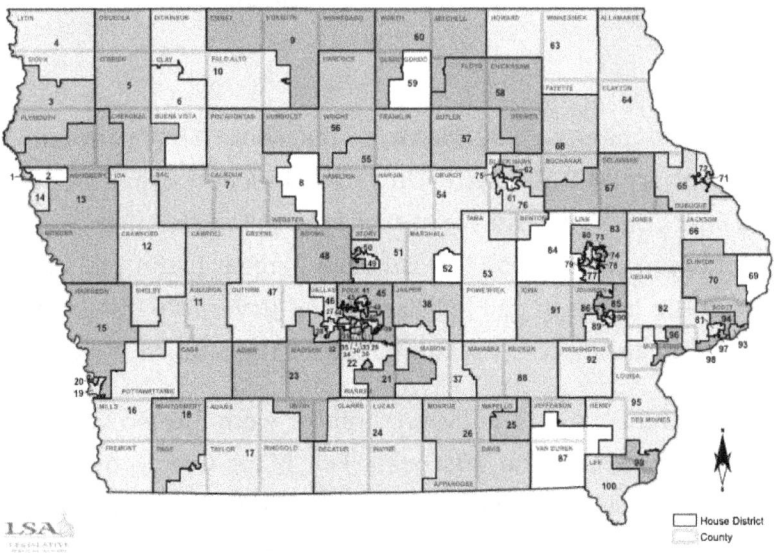

Fairly drawn legislative districts in Iowa. Photo credit: Iowa Legislative Services Agency

The best way to stop gerrymandering is for the legislature to pass legislation that turns over map drawing to an impartial entity, such as a committee of nonpartisan legislative service agencies. It is not unprecedented, as the two state agencies were involved in the map drawing in 1961. This is an Iowa-type plan that fits Wisconsin.

The legislature would have to approve the maps. If they do not, the state agencies mentioned above would redraw them, taking into account the objections if they are presented, then change the maps or send them back to the legislature unchanged. If this kept happening, the third version sent to the legislature would be final, even if the legislature did not adopt the maps. Those would be the maps for the rest of the decade. Simple, clear, and it has a finality to it that a partisan legislature could not stop.

This solution requires a partisan body (the legislature) to give up the power to draw the maps. That's a big ask, as we have found out here in Wisconsin, but I believe this can happen when we have a divided government.

The second best way to end gerrymandering would be to turn the job of drawing maps over to federal judges. This solution worked very well for three decades, from the 1980s to the 2000s.

Why do I suggest federal judges and not state supreme court justices handle this task? Federal judges have lifetime appointments and, therefore, do not have to ever run for re-election. State supreme court justices have to run for re-election every ten years.

I've been around, and I can tell you that re-election is on their minds all ten years of that ten-year term with rare exceptions. This goes for incumbent officeholders, whether they are judges, legislators, or any other elected position in government. This is less true in local elections such as town board, village board, city council, and county board seats. Re-election is about a campaign and campaign dollars and the sources of those dollars. State supreme court justices are well aware of the campaign they ran to successfully get on the court. They remember who supported them, who opposed them, and who provided campaign contributions. I never heard of a justice claiming amnesia regarding all this information.

Just look at what happened in 2022 and 2023. In 2022, a conservative/Republican majority decided 4–3 in favor of a Republican gerrymandered map with "least change" from the 2011 gerrymandered maps. Then the new liberal/Democratic 4–3 majority prepared to redraw the maps in 2023 if the legislature and governor had not agreed on new maps by February 2024 (which they did). Why did the court get involved twice in such a short time? Simply because the philosophical majority changed from a conservative/Republican 4–3 majority to a liberal/Democrat 4–3 majority. I do not believe this is an acceptable route to see repeated in our state's future.

I believe the lifetime appointment of federal judges to their jobs gives them the total freedom to draw fair maps because they do not have to spend one second worrying about whether one party or the other or the major donors like or don't like the maps they draw. We saw the results of this reality when, in 1981, 1991, and 2001, federal judges drew the maps, and there was no gerrymandering. The federal judge solution does presume that the state supreme court does not find a way to allow themselves to draw the maps. It is a no-brainer to me that the drawing of legislative maps could be the permanent job of federal judges if the legislature and governor cannot agree. Getting to this solution is the challenge.

The third best way to end gerrymandering is giving map drawing authority to a commission made up of an equal number of Republicans, Democrats, and independents. This model has been used in other situations over the decades.

Although I have a preference, all three ways would get the job done and end gerrymandering. A large majority of Wisconsin citizens and I will be beyond happy if one of them becomes the solution.

What is the future of gerrymandering in America? I can state my predictions. But people who claim to know for certain are kidding themselves.

One event that could impact the future of gerrymandering is publicizing what just happened in Wisconsin. The news of a Republican legislature passing new maps and Democratic Governor Tony Evers signing them on February 18, 2024, was widely reported across the nation, including stories in the *New York Times* and *Washington Post*. It is highly likely nearly everyone in the United States Congress read about it, and many of their constituents did as well. Many legislators and "fair maps" organizations across America read about it, too.

I cannot predict that gerrymandering across America will decrease or go away. It will take voter education on the issue aided by anti-gerrymander groups in each state. The effort to stop gerrymandering in Wisconsin took 13 years. We must be ever vigilant as total political party control of state government always creates a temptation for legislators. History shows that in many states, this temptation to use their power and gerrymander cannot be resisted.

With no permanent solution, it would be a matter of time before there would be one-party control of state government in the year after the census. This happened in 2011, and Wisconsin got a gerrymander. Then again, in 2021, with divided government and no bipartisan agreement, the state supreme court, with a 4–3 conservative majority (conservative is practically synonymous with Republican, and liberal is practically synonymous with Democrat when it comes to this issue), drew maps under the "least change" theory and issued new maps very similar to the 2011 gerrymandered maps.

The bottom line is that we need a permanent solution, or the value of your vote will always be in doubt, depending on the control of state government or which political philosophy controls the state supreme court.

I do not believe the temptation to gerrymander will ever end. History and the past abuse of power that we've observed confirm this. We need, therefore, to be ever vigilant. Even if we get a system in place that takes the power to draw the maps away from legislators, we will still have to be vigilant. A power taken away from the legislature can be reversed and returned to the legislature.

---

[32] Charles Franklin, "New Marquette Law School Poll Finds Some Issues Less Divisive Amid Continuing Partisan Divide," Marquette University Law School Poll, January 24, 2019, https://law.marquette.edu/poll/author/charles-franklin/page/69/.

CHAPTER 10
America's Future

In politics, this is an age of polarization, often angry polarization. It's unlike any time in my adult life (since 1962). What do we do about this? I'm sure some don't want to do anything about it. But I do, and I believe millions of others do, too.

I believe we need to agree with a shared understanding of what a great country we live in. The last half of the last century saw a pretty broad consensus about America's greatness. We abolished slavery, created national parks, passed laws protecting child labor, created social security, survived the Great Depression, won World War II and defeated Hitler, passed the G.I. Bill, abolished segregation, increased environmental laws, created Medicare and Medicaid, acknowledged the equality of many groups including women, minorities, and people with different sexual preferences. I have certainly not mentioned all, and you will think of some more. There was a broad consensus on all of this, although the popular consensus did not happen overnight on some issues.

It seems today that all of the above is not enough. The generations that lived through so much of it are elderly or have died.

We are Americans. I refuse to believe that we cannot forge a new consensus. I believe it should and could include all of the above. We could start by making sure students who graduate from high school have learned about all of the above.

We could start by using modern tools, obviously led by the internet, to find consensus opinions on issues and not even try to change political party affiliations. This would avoid the need to rely on media reports on the issues because, as we all know, many, many Americans do not trust the media. Maybe there is a consensus out there around the support for one word—*freedom*.

I am writing this book in early 2024. I should note that I wrote this chapter's first paragraphs on December 29, 2017. Our problems today started several years ago. This tells me we need to work harder and faster.

One significant bit of progress would be to end gerrymandering all across America. We have ended it in Wisconsin—hopefully until 2031—but our nation has 49 more states. They do not all have gerrymandered state legislatures or congressional seats, but they could.

I have not focused on congressional gerrymandering. It exists in many states and contributes to our nation's political division.

Freedom certainly means different things to different people. But I believe there must be a consensus on the recognition that Americans have more freedom than literally billions of other people on our planet.

We also need to heed the warnings of Benjamin Franklin. According to the published notes of Dr. James McHenry, a delegate from Maryland attending the Constitutional Convention, Franklin had just participated in the approval of our constitution in Independence Hall in 1787. The public knew that our leaders went there to write and then approve a constitution for our new nation. He was walking down the street in Philadelphia when a woman came up to him and asked, "Well, doctor, what have we got—a republic or a monarchy?"

"A republic," replied the doctor. If you can keep it."[33]

I believe this is one of the most important statements in the history of our nation. It is one of the most important pieces of advice to Americans—and it was said nearly 250 years ago.

Franklin knew nearly 250 years ago that this was the beginning of a great experiment with a country of free white males who could choose their leader. This was great progress compared to the rest of the world, but this freedom to vote left out women, enslaved persons and free African Americans, other people of color, people belonging to certain religions, renters, and Indigenous peoples. Over the next 200-plus years, those groups all eventually had the right to vote. We also lowered the voting age to 18. We are now seeing and feeling what Franklin worried about so long ago.

Our democracy is still a "great experiment," and we must never take it for granted. We are being tested today. We must never forget that we have the greatest experiment in human history. We must always think of it this way and make sure it continues for another 250 years!

I have one idea, maybe more than that. I suggest that no student get out of high school without hearing the above story about Franklin 250 years ago. I admit that as I grew up and for much of my life, I thought that our government and our freedom were a settled matter. That we would always be the greatest, most free nation on Earth. I really never understood that we all had an obligation to make sure it continued to be this "great experiment."

I believe it is worth noting that history teaches us that great, needed change does not come quickly. It can take the better part of 200 or more years. Let's keep trying to get better.

---

[33] The Records of the Federal Convention of 1787, ed. Max Farrand, vol. 3, Appendix A, 85.

ACKNOWLEDGMENTS

"Writing a book is an adventure. To begin with it is a toy and an amusement. Then it becomes a mistress, then it becomes a master, then it becomes a tyrant. The last phase is that just as you are about to be reconciled to your servitude, you kill the monster and fling him out to the public."—Winston Churchill

Like so many of Churchill's quotes, I love this one. I agree that writing a book is an adventure, especially in the sense that research and conversation, along with people knowledgeable about the topic, can inform and change the views you started with, even regarding a subject you believed you knew well.

I don't use terms like "mistress," "master," or "tyrant," but the act of researching this book did instill in me a respect for facts and accuracy as opposed to theories and assumptions, no matter how widely held. I don't refer to this project as "a monster," but I do agree that as I write and write, I reach a point and "give" it to you—not "fling."

I wrote this book myself, just like I did my first two books, *Ringside Seat* and *Disassembled*, but I certainly did not do it alone. Many people helped by sharing details of events, dates, and times and then referring me to others who had firsthand knowledge of various events in the book. I list their names, knowing that I will unintentionally leave out some people. For that, I apologize.

Many, many thanks to my stepdaughter, Erin Jacobson, who typed this entire book from my handwritten pages. My penmanship grades at St. Mary's were never high, and time has not resulted in improvement. Just like with my other books, Erin's contribution went beyond typing. She made many suggestions on changes she thought would make the document clearer. She also gave me much-appreciated advice on some of the content.

My thanks to my friend, Madison journalist and nonfiction author Doug Moe, who has now provided editing assistance on all three of my books. Thanks as well to Kristin Mitchell at Little Creek Press, who has published each of my books.

I am grateful to several people who helped me by referring me to documents that would help me get the information and facts I needed.

Jay Heck, executive director of Common Cause in Wisconsin (where I serve on the board and am a former chair), has been involved in this issue since at least 2009. He is one of the most informed people in Wisconsin on the issue of gerrymandering. He helped me in many ways, especially by referring me to sources that provided key facts when I was aware of an issue but did not have facts and numbers to back up the point I was making. I was only vaguely aware of many events in redistricting going back to before we were a state. Many I was not aware of at all. Jay found sources for me to learn the details.

Matt Rothschild is the author of *12 Ways to Save Democracy in Wisconsin*. His first chapter is titled "Ban Gerrymandering!" He is a longtime friend and the retired executive director of the Wisconsin Democracy Campaign. Chapters one and five of Matt's book were very helpful.

The Wisconsin Legislative Reference Bureau published an extremely informative document entitled "Redistricting in Wisconsin 2020: The LRB Guidebook." The document traces this issue of redistricting to before Wisconsin became a state in 1848.

Michael Gallagher, Joseph Kreye, and Staci Duros, PhD, were the lead authors.

Thanks to my longtime friend and partner in fighting gerrymandering since 2011, Senator Dale Schultz. I devoted a chapter to our joint efforts.

Thanks to The League of Women Voters of Wisconsin for their excellent brochure, "Fair Maps: Representation for All," which I quoted from the brochure. The league was a major player in the coalition that fought to eliminate gerrymandering.

Finally, thanks to the Brennan Center for Justice and its paper entitled, "What States Can Learn from Wisconsin's Win for Fair Maps," published on March 6, 2024.

APPENDIX

Constitution of the United States: Fourteenth Amendment

Section 1. All persons born or naturalized in the United States, and subject to the jurisdiction thereof, are citizens of the United States and of the State wherein they reside. No State shall make or enforce any law which shall abridge the privileges or immunities of citizens of the United States; nor shall any State deprive any person of life, liberty, or property, without due process of law; nor deny to any person within its jurisdiction the equal protection of the laws.

Section 2. Representatives shall be apportioned among the several States according to their respective numbers, counting the whole number of persons in each State, excluding Indians not taxed. But when the right to vote at any election for the choice of electors for President and Vice-President of the United States, Representatives in Congress, the Executive and Judicial officers of a State, or the members of the legislature thereof, is denied to any of the male inhabitants of such State, being twenty-one years of age, and citizens of the United States, or in any way abridged, except for participation in rebellion, or other crime, the basis of representation therein shall be reduced in the proportion which the number of such male citizens shall bear to the whole number of male citizens twenty-one years of age in such State.

Section 3. No person shall be a Senator or Representative in Congress, or elector of President and Vice-President, or hold any office, civil or military, under the United States, or under any State, who, having previously taken an oath, as a member of Congress, or as an officer of the United States, or as a member of any State legislature, or as an executive or judicial officer of any State, to support the Constitution of the United States, shall have engaged in insurrection or rebellion against the same, or given aid or comfort to the enemies thereof. But Congress may by a vote of two-thirds of each House, remove such disability.

Section 4. The validity of the public debt of the United States, authorized by law, including debts incurred for payment of pensions and bounties for services in suppressing insurrection or rebellion, shall not be questioned. But neither the United States nor any State shall assume or pay any debt or obligation incurred in aid of insurrection or rebellion against the United States, or any claim for the loss or emancipation of any slave; but all such debts, obligations and claims shall be held illegal and void.

Section 5. The Congress shall have power to enforce, by appropriate legislation, the provisions of this article.[34]

Constitution of the United States: Fifteenth Amendment

Section 1. The right of citizens of the United States to vote shall not be denied or abridged by the United States or by any State on account of race, color, or previous condition of servitude—

Section 2. The Congress shall have power to enforce this article by appropriate legislation.[35]

Voting Rights Act of 1965

AN ACT To enforce the fifteenth amendment to the Constitution of the United States, and for other purposes. Be it enacted by the Senate and House of Representatives of the United States of America in Congress assembled, That this Act shall be known as the "Voting Rights Act of 1965."

Section 2. No voting qualification or prerequisite to voting, or standard, practice, or procedure shall be imposed or applied by any State or political subdivision to deny or abridge the right of any citizen of the United States to vote on account of race or color.

Section 3. (a) Whenever the Attorney General institutes a proceeding under any statute to enforce the guarantees of the fifteenth amendment in any State or political subdivision the court shall authorize the appointment of Federal examiners by the United States Civil Service Commission in accordance with section 6 to serve for such period of time and for such political subdivisions as the court shall determine is appropriate to enforce the guarantees of the fifteenth amendment (1) as part of any interlocutory order if the court determines that the appointment of such examiners is necessary to enforce such guarantees or (2) as part of any final judgment if the court finds that violations of the fifteenth amendment justifying equitable relief have occurred in such State or subdivision: Provided, That the court need not authorize the appointment of examiners if any incidents of denial or abridgement of the right to vote on account of race or color (1) have been few in number and have been promptly and effectively corrected by State or local action, (2) the continuing effect of such incidents has been eliminated, and (3) there is no reasonable probability of their recurrence in the future.

(b) If in a proceeding instituted by the Attorney General under any statute to enforce the guarantees of the fifteenth amendment in any State or political subdivision the court finds that a test or device has been used for the purpose or with the effect of denying or abridging the right of any citizen of the United States to vote on account of race or color, it shall suspend the use of tests and devices in such State or political subdivisions as the court shall determine is appropriate and for such period as it deems necessary.

(c) If in any proceeding instituted by the Attorney General under any statute to enforce the guarantees of the fifteenth amendment in any State or political subdivision the court finds that violations of the fifteenth amendment justifying equitable relief have occurred within the territory of such State or political subdivision, the court, in addition to such relief as it may grant, shall retain jurisdiction for such period as it may deem appropriate and during such period no voting qualification or prerequisite to voting, or standard, practice, or procedure with respect to voting different from that in force or effect at the time the proceeding was commenced shall be enforced unless and until the court finds that such qualification, prerequisite, standard, practice, or procedure does not have the purpose and will not have the effect of denying or abridging the right to vote on account of race or color: Provided, That such qualification, prerequisite, standard, practice, or procedure may be enforced if the qualification, prerequisite, standard, practice, or procedure has been submitted by the chief legal officer or other appropriate official of such State or subdivision to the Attorney General and the Attorney General has not interposed an objection within sixty days after such submission, except that neither the court's finding nor the Attorney General's failure to object shall bar a subsequent action to enjoin enforcement of such qualification, prerequisite, standard, practice, or procedure.

Section 4. (a) To assure that the right of citizens of the United States to vote is not denied or abridged on account of race or color, no citizen shall be denied the right to vote in any Federal, State, or local election because of his failure to comply with any test or device in any State with respect to which the determinations have been made under subsection (b) or in any political subdivision with respect to which such determinations have been made as a separate unit, unless the United States District Court for the District of Columbia in an action for a declaratory judgment brought by such State or subdivision against the United States has determined that no such test or device has been used during the five years preceding the filing of the action for the purpose or with the effect of denying or abridging the right to vote on account of race or color: Provided, That no such declaratory judgment shall issue with respect to any plaintiff for a period of five years after the entry of a final judgment of any court of the United States, other than the denial of a declaratory judgment under this section, whether entered prior to or after the enactment of this Act, determining that denials or abridgments of the right to vote on account of race or color through the use of such tests or devices have occurred anywhere in the territory of such plaintiff. An action pursuant to this subsection shall be heard and determined by a court of three judges in accordance with the provisions of section 2284 of title 28 of the United States Code and any appeal shall lie to the Supreme Court. The court shall retain jurisdiction of any action pursuant to this subsection for five years after judgment and shall reopen the action upon motion of the Attorney General alleging that a test or device has been used for the purpose or with the effect of denying or abridging the right to vote on account of race or color.

If the Attorney General determines that he has no reason to believe that any such test or device has been used during the five years preceding the filing of the action for the purpose or with the effect of denying or abridging the right to vote on account of race or color, he shall consent to the entry of such judgment.

(b) The provisions of subsection (a) shall apply in any State or in any political subdivision of a state which (1) the Attorney General determines maintained on November 1, 1964, any test or device, and with respect to which (2) the Director of the Census determines that less than 50 percentum of the persons of voting age residing therein were registered on November 1, 1964, or that less than 50 percentum of such persons voted in the presidential election of November 1964.

A determination or certification of the Attorney General or of the Director of the Census under this section or under section 6 or section 13 shall not be reviewable in any court and shall be effective upon publication in the Federal Register.

(c) The phrase "test or device" shall mean any requirement that a person as a prerequisite for voting or registration for voting (1) demonstrate the ability to read, write, understand, or interpret any matter, (2) demonstrate any educational achievement or his knowledge of any particular subject, (3) possess good moral character, or (4) prove his qualifications by the voucher of registered voters or members of any other class.

(d) For purposes of this section no State or political subdivision shall be determined to have engaged in the use of tests or devices for the purpose or with the effect of denying or abridging the right to vote on account of race or color if (1) incidents of such use have been few in number and have been promptly and effectively corrected by State or local action, (2) the continuing effect of such incidents has been eliminated, and (3) there is no reasonable probability of their recurrence in the future.

(e) (1) Congress hereby declares that to secure the rights under the fourteenth amendment of persons educated in American-flag schools in which the predominant classroom language was other than English, it is necessary to prohibit the States from conditioning the right to vote of such persons on ability to read, write, understand, or interpret any matter in the English language. (2) No person who demonstrates that he has successfully completed the sixth primary grade in a public school in, or a private school accredited by, any State or territory, the District of Columbia, or the Commonwealth of Puerto Rico in which the predominant classroom language was other than English, shall be denied the right to vote in any Federal, State, or local election because of his inability to read, write, understand, or interpret any matter in the English language, except that, in States in which State law provides that a different level of education is presumptive of literacy, he shall demonstrate that he has successfully completed an equivalent level of education in a public school in, or a private school accredited by, any State or territory, the District of Columbia, or the Commonwealth of Puerto

Rico in which the predominant classroom language was other than English.

Section 5. Whenever a State or political subdivision with respect to which the prohibitions set forth in section 4(a) are in effect shall enact or seek to administer any voting qualification or prerequisite to voting, or standard, practice, or procedure with respect to voting different from that in force or effect on November 1, 1964, such State or subdivision may institute an action in the United States District Court for the District of Columbia for a declaratory judgment that such qualification, prerequisite, standard, practice, or procedure does not have the purpose and will not have the effect of denying or abridging the right to vote on account of race or color, and unless and until the court enters such judgment no person shall be denied the right to vote for failure to comply with such qualification, prerequisite, standard, practice, or procedure: Provided, That such qualification, prerequisite, standard, practice, or procedure may be enforced without such proceeding if the qualification, prerequisite, standard, practice, or procedure has been submitted by the chief legal officer or other appropriate official of such State or subdivision to the Attorney General and the Attorney General has not interposed an objection within sixty days after such submission, except that neither the Attorney General's failure to object nor a declaratory judgment entered under this section shall bar a subsequent action to enjoin enforcement of such qualification, prerequisite, standard, practice, or procedure. Any action under this section shall be heard and determined by a court of three judges in accordance with the provisions of section 2284 of title 28 of the United States Code and any appeal shall lie to the Supreme Court.

Section 6. Whenever (a) a court has authorized the appointment of examiners pursuant to the provisions of section 3(a), or (b) unless a declaratory judgment has been rendered under section 4(a), the Attorney General certifies with respect to any political subdivision named in, or included within the scope of, determinations made under section 4(b) that (1) he has received complaints in writing from twenty or more residents of such political subdivision alleging that they have been denied the right to vote under color of law on account of race or color, and that he believes such complaints to be meritorious, or (2) that, in his judgment (considering, among other factors, whether the ratio of nonwhite persons to white persons registered to vote within such subdivision appears to him to be reasonably attributable to violations of the fifteenth amendment or whether substantial evidence exists that bona fide efforts are being made within such subdivision to comply with the fifteenth amendment), the appointment of examiners is otherwise necessary to enforce the guarantees of the fifteenth amendment, the Civil Service Commission shall appoint as many examiners for such subdivision as it may deem appropriate to prepare and maintain lists of persons eligible to vote in Federal, State, and local elections. Such examiners, hearing officers provided for in section 9(a), and other persons deemed necessary by the Commission to carry out the provisions and purposes of this Act shall be appointed, compensated, and separated without regard to the provisions of any statute administered by the Civil Service Commission, and service under this Act shall not be considered employment for the purposes of any statute administered by the Civil Service Commission, except the provisions of section 9 of the Act of August 2, 1939, as amended (5 U.S.C. 118i), prohibiting partisan political activity: Provided, That the Commission is authorized, after consulting the head of the appropriate department or agency, to designate suitable persons in the official service of the United States, with their consent, to serve in these positions. Examiners and hearing officers shall have the power to administer oaths.

Section 7. (a) The examiners for each political subdivision shall, at such places as the Civil Service Commission shall by regulation designate, examine applicants concerning their qualifications for voting. An application to an examiner shall be in such form as the Commission may require and shall contain allegations that the applicant is not otherwise registered to vote.

(b) Any person whom the examiner finds, in accordance with instructions received under section 9(b), to have the qualifications prescribed by State law not inconsistent with the Constitution and laws of the United States shall promptly be placed on a list of eligible voters. A challenge to such listing may be made in accordance with section 9(a) and shall not be the basis for a prosecution under section 12 of this Act. The examiner shall certify and transmit such list, and any supplements as appropriate, at least once a month, to the offices of the appropriate election officials, with copies to the Attorney General and the attorney general of the State, and any such lists and supplements thereto transmitted during the month shall be available for public inspection on the last business day of the month and, in any event, not later than the forty-fifth day prior to any election. The appropriate State or local election official shall place such names on the official voting list. Any person whose name appears on the examiner's list shall be entitled and allowed to vote in the election district of his residence unless and until the appropriate election officials shall have been notified that such person has been removed from such list in accordance with subsection (d): Provided, That no person shall be entitled to vote in any election by virtue of this Act unless his name shall have been certified and transmitted on such a list to the offices of the appropriate election officials at least forty-five days prior to such election.

(c) The examiner shall issue to each person whose name appears on such a list a certificate evidencing his eligibility to vote.

(d) A person whose name appears on such a list shall be removed therefrom by an examiner if (1) such person has been successfully challenged in accordance with the procedure prescribed in section 9, or (2) he has been determined by an examiner to have lost his eligibility to vote under State law not inconsistent with the Constitution and the laws of the United States.

Section 8. Whenever an examiner is serving under this Act in any political subdivision, the Civil Service Commission may assign, at the request of the Attorney General, one or more persons, who may be officers of the United States, (1) to enter and attend at any place for holding an election in such subdivision for the purpose of observing whether persons who are entitled to vote are being permitted to vote, and (2) to enter and attend at any place for tabulating the votes cast at any election held in such subdivision for the purpose of observing whether votes cast by persons entitled to vote are being properly tabulated. Such persons so assigned shall report to an examiner appointed for such political subdivision, to the Attorney General, and if the appointment of examiners has been authorized pursuant to section 3(a), to the court.

Section 9. (a) Any challenge to a listing on an eligibility list prepared by an examiner shall be heard and determined by a hearing officer appointed by and responsible to the Civil Service Commission and under such rules as the Commission shall by regulation prescribe. Such challenge shall be entertained only if filed at such office within the State as the Civil Service Commission shall by regulation designate, and within ten days after the listing of the challenged person is made available for public inspection, and if supported by (1) the affidavits of at least two persons having personal knowledge of the facts constituting grounds for the challenge, and (2) a certification that a copy of the challenge and affidavits have been served by mail or in person upon the person challenged at his place of residence set out in the application. Such challenge shall be determined within fifteen days after it has been filed. A petition for review of the decision of the hearing officer may be filed in the United States court of appeals for the circuit in which the person challenged resides within fifteen days after service of such decision by mail on the person petitioning for review but no decision of a hearing officer shall be reversed unless clearly erroneous. Any person listed shall be entitled and allowed to vote pending final determination by the hearing officer and by the court.

(b) The times, places, procedures, and form for application and listing pursuant to this Act and removals from the eligibility lists shall be prescribed by regulations promulgated by the Civil Service Commission and the Commission shall, after consultation with the Attorney General, instruct examiners concerning applicable State law not inconsistent with the Constitution and laws of the United States with respect to (1) the qualifications required for listing, and (2) loss of eligibility to vote.

(c) Upon the request of the applicant or the challenger or on its own motion the Civil Service Commission shall have the power to require by subpoena the attendance and testimony of witnesses and the production of documentary evidence relating to any matter pending before it under the authority of this section. In case of contumacy or refusal to obey a subpoena, any district court of the United States or the United States court of any territory or possession, or the District Court of the United States for the District of Columbia, within the jurisdiction of which said person guilty of contumacy or refusal to obey is found or resides or is domiciled or transacts business, or has appointed an agent for receipt of service of process, upon application by the Attorney General of the United States shall have jurisdiction to issue to such person an order requiring such person to appear before the Commission or a hearing officer, there to produce pertinent, relevant, and nonprivileged documentary evidence if so ordered, or there to give testimony touching the matter under investigation, and any failure to obey such order of the court may be punished by said court as a contempt thereof.

Section 10. (a) The Congress finds that the requirement of the payment of a poll tax as a precondition to voting (i) precludes persons of limited means from voting or imposes unreasonable financial hardship upon such persons as a precondition to their exercise of the franchise, (ii) does not bear a reasonable relationship to any legitimate State interest in the conduct of elections, and (iii) in some areas has the purpose or effect of denying persons the right to vote because of race or color. Upon the basis of these findings, Congress declares that the constitutional right of citizens to vote is denied or abridged in some areas by the requirement of the payment of a poll tax as a precondition to voting.

(b) In the exercise of the powers of Congress under section 5 of the fourteenth amendment and section 2 of the fifteenth amendment, the Attorney General is authorized and directed to institute forthwith in the name of the United States such actions, including actions against States or political subdivisions, for declaratory judgment or injunctive relief against the enforcement of any requirement of the payment of a poll tax as a precondition to voting, or substitute therefor enacted after November 1, 1964, as will be necessary to implement the declaration of subsection (a) and the purposes of this section.

(c) The district courts of the United States shall have jurisdiction of such actions which shall be heard and determined by a court of three judges in accordance with the provisions of section 2284 of title 28 of the United States Code and any appeal shall lie to the Supreme Court. It shall be the duty of the judges designated to hear the case to assign the case for hearing at the earliest practicable date, to participate in the hearing and determination thereof, and to cause the case to be in every way expedited.

(d) During the pendency of such actions, and thereafter if the courts, notwithstanding this action by the Congress, should declare the requirement of the payment of a poll tax to be constitutional, no citizen of the United States who is a resident of a State or political subdivision with respect to which determinations have been made under subsection 4(b) and a declaratory judgment has not been entered under subsection 4(a), during the first year he becomes otherwise entitled to vote by reason of registration by State or local officials or listing by an examiner, shall be denied the right to vote for failure to pay a poll tax if he tenders payment of such tax for the current year to an examiner or to the appropriate State or local official at least forty-five days prior to election, whether or not such tender would be timely or adequate under State law. An examiner shall have authority to accept such payment from any person authorized by this Act to make an application for listing, and shall issue a receipt for such payment. The examiner shall transmit promptly any such poll tax payment to the office of the State or local official authorized to receive such payment under State law, together with the name and address of the applicant.

Section 11. (a) No person acting under color of law shall fail or refuse to permit any person to vote who is entitled to vote under any provision of this Act or is otherwise qualified to vote, or willfully fail or refuse to tabulate, count, and report such person's vote.

(b) No person, whether acting under color of law or otherwise, shall intimidate, threaten, or coerce, or attempt to intimidate, threaten, or coerce any person for voting or attempting to vote, or intimidate, threaten, or coerce, or attempt to intimidate, threaten, or coerce any person for urging or aiding any person to vote or attempt to vote, or intimidate, threaten, or coerce any person for exercising any powers or duties under section 3(a), 6, 8, 9, 10, or 12(e).

(c) Whoever knowingly or willfully gives false information as to his name, address, or period of residence in the voting district for the purpose of establishing his eligibility to register or vote, or conspires with another individual for the purpose of encouraging his false registration to vote or illegal voting, or pays or offers to pay or accepts payment either for registration to vote or for voting shall be fined not more than $10,000 or imprisoned not more than five years, or both: Provided, however, That this provision shall be applicable only to general, special, or primary elections held solely or in part for the purpose of selecting or electing any candidate for the office of President, Vice President, presidential elector, Member of the United States Senate, Member of the United States House of Representatives, or Delegates or Commissioners from the territories or possessions, or Resident Commissioner of the Commonwealth of Puerto Rico.

(d) Whoever, in any matter within the jurisdiction of an examiner or hearing officer knowingly and willfully falsifies or conceals a material fact, or makes any false, fictitious, or fraudulent statements or representations, or makes or uses any false writing or document knowing the same to contain any false, fictitious, or fraudulent statement or entry, shall be fined not more than $10,000 or imprisoned not more than five years, or both.

Section 12. (a) Whoever shall deprive or attempt to deprive any person of any right secured by section 2, 3, 4, 5, 7, or 10 or shall violate section 11(a) or (b), shall be fined not more than $5,000, or imprisoned not more than five years, or both.

(b) Whoever, within a year following an election in a political subdivision in which an examiner has been appointed (1) destroys, defaces, mutilates, or otherwise alters the marking of a paper ballot which has been cast in such election, or (2) alters any official record of voting in such election tabulated from a voting machine or otherwise, shall be fined not more than $5,000, or imprisoned not more than five years, or both.

(c) Whoever conspires to violate the provisions of subsection (a) or (b) of this section, or interferes with any right secured by section 2, 3 4, 5, 7, 10, or 11(a) or (b) shall be fined not more than $5,000, or imprisoned not more than five years, or both.

(d) Whenever any person has engaged or there are reasonable grounds to believe that any person is about to engage in any act or practice prohibited by section 2, 3, 4, 5, 7, 10, 11, or subsection (b) of this section, the Attorney General may institute for the United States, or in the name of the United States, an action for preventive relief, including an application for a temporary or permanent injunction, restraining order, or other order, and including an order directed to the State and State or local election officials to require them (1) to permit persons listed under this Act to vote and (2) to count such votes.

(e) Whenever in any political subdivision in which there are examiners appointed pursuant to this Act any persons allege to such an examiner within forty-eight hours after the closing of the polls that notwithstanding (1) their listing under this Act or registration by an appropriate election official and (2) their eligibility to vote, they have not been permitted to vote in such election, the examiner shall forthwith notify the Attorney General if such allegations in his opinion appear to be well founded. Upon receipt of such notification, the Attorney General may forthwith file with the district court an application for an order providing for the marking, casting, and counting of the ballots of such persons and requiring the inclusion of their votes in the total vote before the results of such election shall be deemed final and any force or effect given thereto. The district court shall hear and determine such matters immediately after the filing of such application. The remedy provided in this subsection shall not preclude any remedy available under State or Federal law.

(f) The district courts of the United States shall have jurisdiction of proceedings instituted pursuant to this section and shall exercise the same without regard to whether a person asserting rights under the provisions of this Act shall have exhausted any administrative or other remedies that may be provided by law.

Section 13. Listing procedures shall be terminated in any political subdivision of any State (a) with respect to examiners appointed pursuant to clause (b) of section 6 whenever the Attorney General notifies the Civil Service Commission, or whenever the District Court for the District of Columbia determines in an action for declaratory judgment brought by any political subdivision with respect to which the Director of the Census has determined that more than 50 percentum of the nonwhite persons of voting age residing therein are registered to vote, (1) that all persons listed by an examiner for such subdivision have been placed on the appropriate voting registration roll, and (2) that there is no longer reasonable cause to believe that persons will be deprived of or denied the right to vote on account of race or color in such subdivision, and (b), with respect to examiners appointed pursuant to section 3(a), upon order of the authorizing court. A political subdivision may petition the Attorney General for the termination of listing procedures under clause (a) of this section, and may petition the Attorney General to request the Director of the Census to take such survey or census as may be appropriate for the making of the determination provided for in this section. The District Court for the District of Columbia shall have jurisdiction to require such survey or census to be made by the Director of the Census and it shall require him to do so if it deems the Attorney General's refusal to request such survey or census to be arbitrary or unreasonable.

Section 14. (a) All cases of criminal contempt arising under the provisions of this Act shall be governed by section 151 of the Civil Rights Act of 1957 (42 U.S.C.1995).

(b) No court other than the District Court for the District of Columbia or a court of appeals in any proceeding under section 9 shall have jurisdiction to issue any declaratory judgment pursuant to section 4 or section 5 or any restraining order or temporary or permanent injunction against the execution or enforcement of any provision of this Act or any action of any Federal officer or employee pursuant hereto.

(c) (1) The terms "vote" or "voting" shall include all action necessary to make a vote effective in any primary, special, or general election, including, but not limited to, registration, listing pursuant to this Act, or other action required by law prerequisite to voting, casting a ballot, and having such ballot counted properly and included in the appropriate totals of votes cast with respect to candidates for public or party office and propositions for which votes are received in an election. (2) The term "political subdivision" shall mean any county or parish, except that, where registration for voting is not conducted under the supervision of a county or parish, the term shall include any other subdivision of a State which conducts registration for voting.

(d) In any action for a declaratory judgment brought pursuant to section 4 or section 5 of this Act, subpoenas for witnesses who are required to attend the District Court for the District of Columbia may be served in any judicial district of the United States: Provided, That no writ of subpoena shall issue for witnesses without the District of Columbia at a greater distance than one hundred miles from the place of holding court without the permission of the District Court for the District of Columbia being first had upon proper application and cause shown.

Section 15. Section 2004 of the Revised Statutes (42 U.S.C.1971), as amended by section 131 of the Civil Rights Act of 1957 (71 Stat. 637), and amended by section 601 of the Civil Rights Act of 1960 (74 Stat. 90), and as further amended by section 101 of the Civil Rights Act of 1964 (78 Stat. 241), is further amended as follows:

(a) Delete the word "Federal" wherever it appears in subsections (a) and (c);

(b) Repeal subsection (f) and designate the present subsections (g) and (h) as (f) and (g), respectively.

Section 16. The Attorney General and the Secretary of Defense, jointly, shall make a full and complete study to determine whether, under the laws or practices of any State or States, there are preconditions to voting, which might tend to result in discrimination against citizens serving in the Armed Forces of the United States seeking to vote. Such officials shall, jointly, make a report to the Congress not later than June 30, 1966, containing the results of such study, together with a list of any States in which such preconditions exist, and shall include in such report such recommendations for legislation as they deem advisable to prevent discrimination in voting against citizens serving in the Armed Forces of the United States.

Section 17. Nothing in this Act shall be construed to deny, impair, or otherwise adversely affect the right to vote of any person registered to vote under the law of any State or political subdivision.

Section 18. There are hereby authorized to be appropriated such sums as are necessary to carry out the provisions of this Act.

Section 19. If any provision of this Act or the application thereof to any person or circumstances is held invalid, the remainder of the Act and the application of the provision to other persons not similarly situated or to other circumstances shall not be affected thereby.

Approved August 6, 1965.[36]

Bowman v. Dammann (1932) Case Summary

Original action for an injunction by the State of Wisconsin on the relation of George A. Bowman against Theo. Dammann, Secretary of State—[By Editorial Staff]

Injunction denied, and the complaint dismissed.

Original Action. This action was commenced in this court permanently to enjoin and restrain the defendant, as Secretary of State, from taking any action or, in any manner, proceeding in the matter of any election to be held in this state in the year 1932, for the offices of Assembly or Senate in the districts attempted to be created by chapter 27, Special Session Laws of 1931–32, which purports to reapportion the legislative districts of the state, and from, in any manner, executing any duties arising out of, or based upon, the provisions of this chapter, for the reason that the law as enacted is unconstitutional and void.[37]

State ex rel. Attorney General v. Cunningham (1892) Case Summary

The State ex rel. Attorney General v. Cunningham 81 Wis. 440 (1892) and *The State ex rel. Lamb v. Cunningham* 83 Wis. 90 (1892)

From the time Wisconsin gained statehood, there have been various power struggles among the three branches of government. These cases involved a dispute between the Wisconsin Supreme Court and the Legislature. The Supreme Court held that an act to apportion and district the members of the state Senate and Assembly was unconstitutional. The first decision was unanimous and Justice Harlow S. Orton wrote the opinion. In the second case, a split court reaffirmed the principles set forth in the first decision. Justice John B. Cassoday wrote the majority opinion. Justice John B. Winslow dissented.

In these cases, the court outlawed "gerrymandering," which is creating legislative districts to preserve partisan political advantage.

Article IV of the Wisconsin Constitution provides that every ten years the Legislature shall "apportion and district anew" the members of the Senate and Assembly, according to the number of inhabitants in each district. Assembly districts are to be bounded by county, precinct, town or ward lines, to consist of contiguous territory (that is, a block of land rather than islands here and there) and be as compact as practicable. Senators are to be elected by single districts of convenient, contiguous territory. No Assembly district may follow the same exact lines as a Senate district.

In the first case, the attorney general appeared on behalf of the state to ask the Court to stop the secretary of state from giving the notices of the election for members of the Senate and Assembly under the new apportionment act. The attorney general argued that the apportionment act violated the constitutional provisions discussed above because:

- districts were not drawn according to the number of inhabitants;
- many Assembly districts were not bounded by county, precinct, town or ward lines;
- many districts were not as compact as practicable and
- some Senate districts did not consist of convenient contiguous territories. The lawyer representing the secretary of state argued that the attorney general had no authority to challenge the law and that only a person who has suffered an actual injury to himself, his property or rights may make such a challenge. The attorney general argued that the question involved was one of public right in which all the citizens of the state were concerned and that the person bringing the suit need not have any individual interest.

The Supreme Court concluded that since the issues raised were of concern to the general public, the attorney general was right to bring the case. The Court then found the act unconstitutional.

After the first decision, the Legislature reconvened and passed another apportionment law. This time, a private citizen asked the Supreme Court to stop the secretary of state from giving notice of the election.

The majority of the court held that the private citizen also had a right to bring the action and that the apportionment law was again unconstitutional. While the first law had formed assembly districts that crossed county lines, the second law created districts with a significant disparity in population. The majority explained:

The requirement that assembly districts must be as nearly equal in population as the other constitutional provisions will permit is just as applicable to two or more assembly districts in a single county as to an assembly district composed of two or more counties. While the act here in question in the main conforms to those requirements of the constitution which prevent equality of representation, yet it almost wholly disregarded the only constitutional requirement particularly designed to secure such equality as near as practicable. (emphasis added)

Justice Winslow dissented, saying he would conclude that the private party who brought the suit had no right to sue because he had suffered no wrong as a result of the law. He also said he did not believe the disparity in population between the districts was significant enough to render the act unconstitutional. Winslow said he feared the Court was entering into a period in which the Legislature would keep enacting laws and the Court would keep striking them down. He wrote: "By the time this process has been repeated several times more, it will be a serious question whether the law finally resulting is the offspring of the legislature or of the court... Has not the court in fact made the law, and thus invaded the province of its coordinate branch of the government?"[38]

Thornburg v. Gingles (1986)
June 30, 1986
Case Summary

After the North Carolina General Assembly enacted a new legislative redistricting plan in 1982, several African American voters filed a federal lawsuit alleging that one single-member district and six multi-member districts were drawn to impair the ability of African American voters to elect candidates of their choice in violation of Section 2 of the Voting Rights Act. After the plaintiffs filed suit, but before trial, Congress enacted the 1982 Amendments to the Voting Rights Act overturning the Court's ruling in *City of Mobile v. Alabama* by clarifying that a racial discrimination claim under Section 2 could be established by showing an election law has either a discriminatory purpose or a discriminatory effect. The 1982 Amendments also articulated a list of factors for courts to consider when evaluating whether an election law has a discriminatory effect under the "totality of circumstances."

In 1986, the U.S. Supreme Court held that four of the state's multi-member districts violated Section 2 and, in its unanimous opinion, the Court discussed the legal impact of the 1982 Amendments to the Voting Rights Act for the first time. Recognizing that multi-member districts have the potential to be used to dilute the voting strength of minority populations in certain situations, the Court articulated three preconditions that a plaintiff challenging multi-member districts under Section 2 must prove in order to prevail on their claim: First, the minority voting group is sufficiently large and geographically compact such that it could constitute a voting majority in a single-member district if it were drawn; Second, the minority group is politically cohesive (i.e. votes similarly); and Third, the majority racial group in the district usually votes as a bloc so as to defeat the minority's preferred candidate. Only after the plaintiff establishes these three conditions may the Court proceed to analyze whether, under the "totality of circumstances" factors in the 1982 VRA Amendments, the electoral and political process as challenged is equally open to minority voters. The Court also confirmed that pursuant to the 1982 Amendments, plaintiffs do not need to establish discriminatory intent or purpose to prevail on a vote dilution claim under Section 2. Applying those newly established standards to the facts and circumstances in this case, the Court found that in each of the offending districts there was a history of racially polarized voting; a legacy of official discrimination in voting matters, education, housing, employment, and health services; and consistent appeals by campaigns to racial prejudice, which acted in concert with the multi-member district scheme to impair the ability of African American voters to participate equally in the political process and to elect candidates of their choice.

Significance: Under the 1982 Amendments to the Voting Rights Act, Section 2 requires that multi-member districts be broken into minority single-member districts only where 3 pre-conditions are shown: (1) the minority group is sufficiently large and compact such that it can comprise the majority of a single-member district if drawn; (2) the minority group is politically cohesive, and (3) the majority usually votes as a block so as to defeat the minority's choice for representative. If all three preconditions are shown, the court must consider the totality of circumstances to determine whether the political process is equally open to minority voters. Plaintiffs no longer need to establish discriminatory intent or purpose to prevail on a vote dilution claim under Section 2.[39]

Baker v. Carr (1962)
Case Summary

Baker v. Carr (1962) is the U.S. Supreme Court case that held that federal courts could hear cases alleging that a state's drawing of electoral boundaries, i.e. redistricting, violates the Equal Protection Clause of the Fourteenth Amendment of the Constitution. In so ruling, the Court also reformulated the political question doctrine. Find the full text of the case here.

In the case, the plaintiff lived in an urban Tennessee voting district which was relatively underrepresented compared to rural voting districts. Tennessee law required districts to be redrawn every ten years, but Tennessee had not done so in decades. The plaintiff sued in federal district court, claiming that the law required Tennessee to redraw their districts to make each district's representation substantially equal to its population. The lower court held it was a political question and therefore non-justiciable, dismissing plaintiff's case. The U.S. Supreme Court disagreed and held that the constitutionality of a legislative appointment scheme was not a political question and therefore was justiciable; i.e., a federal court could hear the case and decide on the merits.

In finding this case justiciable, the Court created the political question doctrine, which creates a series of factors, at least one of which must be present, in order for the case to be a non-justiciable political question. Under the doctrine, if any of the following are met, then the court may not hear the case: (a) commitment of the issue to a branch of government other than the judiciary; (b) lack of standards for resolving the issue; (c) impossibility of the judiciary to resolve the issue without first making a policy determination; (d) a judicial decision of that matter as a lack of respect for other branches of government; (e) a political decision has already been made; or (f) the potential for multiple pronouncements by various branches on one question.

Further, by holding that such cases were justiciable, the Supreme Court paved the way for federal courts to hear and decide on claims that electoral districts violated the equal protection clause. Two years later, the U.S. Supreme Court relied on Baker to require that the United States House of Representatives and state legislatures establish electoral districts of equal population in *Wesberry v. Sanders* and *Reynolds v. Sims*. Future cases also invoked Baker's formulation of the political question doctrine, such as *Nixon v. United States*.[40]

Gill v. Whitford (2016)
Case Summary

In November 2016, the panel declared that the state house plan adopted by Wisconsin's Republican-controlled legislature in 2011 was an unconstitutional partisan gerrymander that violated both the Equal Protection Clause and the plaintiffs' First Amendment freedom of association. The ruling was the first time in over three decades that a federal court invalidated a redistricting plan for partisan bias.

After evaluating the constitutionality of the map with a three-part test, the panel concluded that the map displayed both bad intent and bad effect, citing evidence that the map drawers used special partisan measurements to ensure that the map maximized Republican advantages in assembly seats. Despite Democrats winning a majority of the statewide assembly vote in 2012 and 2014, Republicans won sixty of the ninety-nine assembly seats. Wisconsin Republicans dispute the assertion that they intentionally engineered a biased map, arguing that partisan skews in the map reflect a natural geographic advantage they have in redistricting as a result of Democrats clustering in cities while Republicans are spread out more evenly throughout the state. The court, however, said the state's natural political geography "does not explain adequately the sizeable disparate effect" seen in the previous two election cycles.

Wisconsin filed an appeal on February 24, 2017, asking the Supreme Court to review the decision striking down the map. On June 18, the Court dismissed the case for lack of standing and remanded the case to the district court for further proceedings. On remand, the district court permitted the Wisconsin State Assembly to intervene as defendants in the case.

On January 23, 2019, the court granted in part the State assembly's motion to stay the case, postponing trial until the U.S. Supreme Court ruled on partisan gerrymandering appeals from North Carolina and Maryland on June 27, 2019. The Supreme Court's opinion in those cases held that partisan gerrymandering claims are nonjusticiable. On July 2, 2019, the court dismissed the case.[41]

Lamone v. Benisek (2013)
Case Summary

Plaintiffs filed a complaint in the U.S. District Court for the District of Maryland on November 5, 2013 challenging the congressional redistricting plan enacted by the Maryland General Assembly following the 2010 Census. In the complaint, plaintiffs claimed the district plan was a partisan gerrymander which violated the right to representation guaranteed by Article 1 Section 2 of the U.S.

Constitution, and the First Amendment's protection of political association.

A district judge dismissed the case in April 2014 for failure to state a claim, but did so without convening a three-judge panel. The U.S. Court of Appeals for the Fourth Circuit summarily affirmed the lower court's decision not to convene a three-judge panel, and the plaintiffs appealed to the U.S. Supreme Court.

On December 8, 2015, the Supreme Court unanimously rejected the decisions of the lower courts, holding that they had been too dismissive of the plaintiffs' partisan gerrymandering claims. Writing for the Court, Justice Antonin Scalia stated that the law "could not be clearer" in requiring that a three-judge panel be convened in cases challenging a statewide district plan. The only exceptions to the rule are the rare cases where a claim is "essentially fictitious" or "obviously frivolous." The Court said the partisan gerrymandering claims in the Maryland case, which were based in part on First Amendment theories of liability, "easily cleared [that] low bar."

Plaintiffs' claims center on the unconstitutionality of Maryland's 6th Congressional District, in which voters elected a Republican in the 2010 election but which has consistently been represented by a Democrat since it was redrawn in 2011.

On August 24, 2016, the three-judge panel issued a 2–1 opinion denying the state defendants' motion to dismiss the case, and the parties proceeded with pretrial discovery.

On May 31, 2017 the plaintiffs filed a motion for preliminary injunction or, in the alternative, summary judgment. The state filed a cross-motion for summary judgment and opposed the plaintiffs' motion for preliminary injunction on June 30.

On August 24, the district court denied the plaintiffs' request for an injunction blocking use of the maps. The court also entered an order staying any further proceedings in the case pending a decision by the Supreme Court in *Gill v. Whitford*. The plaintiffs filed an appeal on August 25 asking the Supreme Court to review the decision not to enjoin the map.

The Supreme Court heard oral argument in the case on March 28, 2018.

On June 18, 2018, the Court affirmed the district court's decision not to enjoin the map, holding that the district court's denial was not abuse of discretion.

On remand, the district court heard oral argument on the plaintiffs' motion for summary judgment on October 4, 2018.

On November 7, 2018, the court granted the plaintiffs' request to permanently block further use of the 2011 plan and ordered new maps be drawn for the 2020 elections. The court ruled that it will appoint a three-person commission headed by a magistrate judge to redraw the congressional map if the state does not submit a valid plan by March 7, 2019.

On November 15, 2018, the defendants appealed the panel's decision to the U.S. Supreme Court, and on November 16, secured a stay of the panel's order pending appeal. On January 4, 2019, the Supreme Court agreed to hear the defendants' appeal. The Court heard oral argument on March 26.

On June 27, 2019, the Court vacated the decision below and remanded the case for dismissal, holding that partisan gerrymandering claims are nonjusticiable. On August 9, 2019, the court dismissed the case for lack of jurisdiction.[42]

34 U.S. Constitution, amend. 14.

35 U.S. Constitution, amend. 15.

36 "Voting Rights Act (1965)," Milestone Documents, National Archives, accessed June 18, 2024, https://www.archives.gov/milestone-documents/voting-rights-act.

37 *State ex rel. Bowman v. Barczak*, 34 Wis. 2d 57 (1967), https://law.justia.com/cases/wisconsin/supreme-court/1967/34-wis-2d-57-6.html.

38 "The State ex rel. Attorney General v. Cunningham 81 Wis. 440 (1892) and *The State ex rel. Lamb v. Cunningham* 83 Wis. 90 (1891), https://www.wicourts.gov/courts/supreme/docs/famouscases12.pdf.

39 "*Thornburg v. Gingles* (1986)," The American Redistricting Project, June 30, 1986, https://thearp.org/litigation/thornburg-v-gingles/.

40 "*Baker v. Carr* (1962)," Legal Information Institute, https://www.law.cornell.edu/wex/baker_v_carr_(1962).

41 "*Gill v. Whitford*," Brennan Center for Justice, July 3, 2019 https://www.brennancenter.org/our-work/court-cases/gill-v-whitford.

42 "Lamone v. Benisek," Brennan Center for Justice, July 29, 2019, https://www.brennancenter.org/oour-work/court-cases/lamone-v-benisek.

BIBLIOGRAPHY

"*Baker v. Carr (1962)*," Legal Information Institute, https://www.law.cornell.edu/wex/baker_v_carr_(1962).

Farrand, Max, ed. The Records of the Federal Convention of 1787, ed. Max Farrand, New Haven, Yale University Press, 1911.

Franklin, Charles. "New Marquette Law School Poll Finds Some Issues Less Divisive Amid Continuing Partisan Divide," Marquette University Law School Poll, January 24, 2019, https://law.marquette.edu/poll/author/charles-franklin/page/69/.

Gallagher, Michael, Joseph Kreye, and Staci Duros, PhD, "Redistricting in Wisconsin 2020: The LRB Guidebook," Wisconsin Legislative Reference Bureau, 2020.

"*Gill v. Whitford*," Brennan Center for Justice, July 3, 2019, https://www.brennancenter.org/our-work/court-cases/gill-v-whitford.

Keane, Michael. "Redistricting in Wisconsin," Wisconsin Legislative Reference Bureau, April 1, 2016, https://www.wisdc.org/images/files/pdf_imported/redistricting/redistricting_april2016_leg_ref_bureau.pdf.

"*Lamone v. Benisek*," Brennan Center for Justice, July 29, 2019, https://www.brennancenter.org/our-work/court-cases/lamone-v-benisek.

League of Women Voters, *Fair Maps: Representation for All* (Brochure).

Marquette University Law School Research Fellow John Johnson.

Miller, Peter, "What States Can Learn from Wisconsin's Win for Fair Maps," Brennan Center for Justice, March 6, 2024, https://www.brennancenter.org/our-work/research-reports/what-states-can-learn-wisconsins-win-fair-maps.

The Records of the Federal Convention of 1787, ed. Max Farrand, vol. 3, Appendix A, 85.

Rothschild, Matt. *Twelve Ways to Save Democracy in Wisconsin*. Wisconsin: University of Wisconsin Press, 2021.

"*The State ex rel. Attorney General v. Cunningham* 81 Wis. 440 (1892) and *The State ex rel. Lamb v. Cunningham*," 83 Wis. 90 (1891)," https://www.wicourts.gov/courts/supreme/docs/famouscases12.pdf.

"*State ex rel. Bowman v. Barczak*," 34 Wis. 2d 57 (1967), https://law.justia.com/cases/wisconsin/supreme-court/1967/34-wis-2d-57-6.html.

"*Thornburg v. Gingles* (1986)," The American Redistricting Project, June 30, 1986, https://thearp.org/litigation/thornburg-v-gingles/.

Trickey, Erick, "Where Did the Term 'Gerrymandering' Come From?" *Smithsonian* Magazine, July 20, 2017, https://www.smithsonianmag.com/history/where-did-term-gerrymander-come-180964118/.

U.S. Constitution, amend. 14.

U.S. Constitution, amend. 15.

"Voting Rights Act (1965)," Milestone Documents, National Archives, accessed June 18, 2024, https://www.archives.gov/milestone-documents/voting-rights-act.

"Waupun Correctional Institution Maximum," June 20, 2023, State of Wisconsin Department of Corrections, https://doc.wi.gov/DataResearch/DataAndReports/WCIInstitutionalFactSheet.pdf.

Wisconsin Department of Corrections, DOC-302, "Persons in Our Care," https://doc.wi.gov/DataResearch/WeeklyPopulationReports/06142024.pdf.

Wisconsin Legislative Reference Bureau, LRB Reports, "Salaries of State Elected Officials, 2023," February 2023, https://docs.legis.wisconsin.gov/misc/lrb/lrb_reports/elected_official_salaries_2023_7_5.pdf.

www.ingramcontent.com/pod-product-compliance
Lightning Source LLC
LaVergne TN
LVHW051550300125
802574LV00005B/669